New Life SERIES

Dare to Be Different

By Stephen D. Hower

CPH
Concordia Publishing House

Edited by Thomas J. Doyle

Copyright © 1998 Concordia Publishing House
3558 S. Jefferson Avenue, St. Louis, MO 63118-3968
Manufactured in the United States of America

3 4 5 6 7 8 9 10   07 06 05 04 03 02 01 00

Contents

In Honor of
Don Olson Sr.
Who Taught by Example

Foreword

Always be ready to make your defense to anyone who demands from you an accounting for the hope that is in you.
1 Peter 3:15 NRSV

"Always be ready." Those are important words. They provide at least three important learnings. First, it is possible to be ready to share our faith. Second, you never know when the faith-sharing opportunity will arise, so readiness is the order of the day. Third, people need help and encouragement in that readiness.

This book is meant to be a tool for the Christian's readiness. It gives wise and practical steps for the Christian to take. You will find your time spent pondering and applying its points very productive in your own witness to Jesus Christ. All of us are called upon to be witnesses for Jesus Christ. 1 Peter 2:9–10 says all Christians by virtue of their Baptism are priests called to declare the mighty works of God. Acts 1:8 calls God's people witnesses. It is our duty and delight.

Congregations are finding that evangelism is not a program; though programmatic emphases can assist evangelism. Evangelism is not an event; though certain events can assist members in sharing their faith. Evangelism is a lifestyle. George Barna, head of Barna Research Group and an astute watcher of the churched and unchurched scene in America, writes that evangelistic congregations have this characteristic: "Their definition of success in evangelism is that people active in the church are intentionally and obediently sharing their faith with nonbelievers" (*Evangelism That Works*, p. 92). In other words, evangelism is sharing Christ in the daily life of the believer. It is a lifestyle.

Yet there is need for congregations to be more intentional about the task of helping their members "always be prepared." According to the Barna Research Group, only 12 percent of pastors could say their parishioners are effectively prepared to witness; 85 percent of the Christians who actively witness said they would

7

like to be better trained in evangelism. This book can be a valuable resource in that training.

A Partnership

This book represents a partnership between Concordia Publishing House and the Department of Evangelism Ministry of the Board for Congregational Services. Our goal is to work together to supply congregations and individuals with timely, effective, and faithful resources for training in evangelism. This book is one of a series in which the two entities are cooperating.

How to Use this Book

We hope that this book will be helpful in a variety of settings.

A weekly Bible class could take a number of weeks and work through this course. The text could be read ahead of time, reviewed in class, and the discussion questions could guide the class discussion.

A small group/home group could study this book over a period of meetings. This would be an excellent setting in which to take the time to encourage one another and support one another as participants take practical steps to be witnesses to Christ.

Two Christian friends could covenant to study this book together. They could help and encourage each other. Perhaps, most important, they could hold one another accountable to the learning and doing involved in this class.

Also, an individual could read, study, ponder, and apply the learnings of this book by herself or himself.

Congregations working hard at equipping their members for evangelism will find many more ways to use this book.

Words of Appreciation

What a joy it has been to work with Concordia Publishing House and Stephen Hower on this project. We commend them for work well done. A special thanks to Steve for the fine work he did in writing these chapters. They reflect discussions from a daylong meeting and add creativity and personal touches to the notes of that day. Also, thanks to Rodney Rathmann at Concordia Publishing House for the work he has done and is doing in bringing this evangelism series into being.

It is our prayer that many will be blessed by their time in this book. Above all, we pray that all of us will grow in bold witness to our wonderful Savior, that many would come to trust His grace and that all glory will go to Him.

Rev. Jerry M. Kosberg, *Director*
Department of Evangelism Ministry
Board for Congregational Services
The Lutheran Church—Missouri Synod

Introduction

"No-Threat Christians"

Gen. Douglas MacArthur was visiting the troops on the front lines in Korea. The famous general had been discouraged from visiting a particular site because of its proximity to enemy troops. But in predictable fashion, MacArthur insisted that the troops needed to see their commander. Sure enough, as the entourage moved along the line, shots rang out and bullets came whizzing into the camp. The general and his detachment dove into a bunker, where he grabbed a bewhiskered sergeant and ordered that he form a squad and find that sniper.

"Oh, sir," the sergeant responded. "That won't be necessary. We know exactly where he's located."

"Then why hasn't someone taken him out?" demanded the general.

"Well sir, he's been sniping this hill for six weeks and hasn't hit anyone yet. We're afraid if we take him out the enemy might replace him with someone who can actually shoot!"

Many Christians have been living their lives like that sniper. They have all the equipment, know their job, but have been frustratingly ineffective at the task of Christian witnessing. Satan needn't concern himself with these hidden lights lest they be replaced by another ... one that might actually reflect the light of Christ more openly. This book is written to provide Christian models of encouragement and practical suggestions for those who desire to be more faithful in their witness. It is based on the proposition that every Christian has the potential to be a powerful witness. When Christians share Christ with those within their sphere of influence, the Holy Spirit goes to work. Faith shared is a powerful thing. Even faith the size of a mustard seed, when shared, can make an eternal difference in the lives of the lost and those who love them. By the law of contrast, even a match struck in a dark place is readily seen and quickly draws the attention of all around.

INTRODUCTION

There is good reason for Christians to live more boldly their faith before a nonbelieving world. We are reminded in God's Word that no Christian witnesses alone. The power to bring the lost to Christ is bound solely in God's means of grace—the power of His Word. We are equipped with a powerful weapon against the forces of evil. God's mysterious and powerful Word can never be rendered ineffectual but goes forth with the power of His Spirit. A separate chapter is included which discusses the nature of the living Word and how as Christians we can better wield the sword of the Lord. This work is dedicated to the command of Christ in His sermon on the mount, "Let your light shine before men in such a way that they may see your good works, and glorify your Father who is in heaven" (Matthew 5:16 NASB). As the salt and light of the world we must **_dare to be different!_**

Session 1
Only a Christian

Roy is a good friend of mine and has been so for almost 10 years. His father deserted his family when Roy was just a baby. Unable to support five children, Roy's mother also gave up. Jotting a letter explaining her troubles, she pinned it and the future of her family to the door of a Christian pastor. The pastor and his wife found homes for all of the children but raised Roy as their own son. Roy grew up troubled and in trouble most of the time. He eventually ran away from home, drifted from state to state, got married, then divorced and finally, in no uncertain terms hit bottom—and hit it hard.

Although Roy had forgotten the Lord, the Lord had never forgotten Roy. When he found himself spending the night under a bridge in St. Louis with only a few pennies to his name, Roy called out to the Lord, who happened to be nearby. Since that day Roy's life has continued to be a bold adventure—only this time, an adventure that has been led by the Spirit of the Lord.

God blessed Roy. He married a faithful Christian, and together they achieved success in business and established a happy family. But a stable family, beautiful home, and success in business was not enough. Roy wanted his life to have eternal consequence. He became increasingly involved in his local congregation, serving on various boards and committees. But committee work didn't really satisfy Roy's need to help others in crisis. So Roy completed an extensive course in peer counseling, volunteered as chaplain's assistant at a local hospital, and began to accept invitations to share the story of his faith-walk at various places, including Christian high schools, the county jail, Christian congregations, as a chaplain at a race track (where he races his car in the quarter-mile drag competition), and at numerous Christian businessmen's gatherings around the city. Roy was ready, or so he thought, to enter a more intentional ministry. He was determined to leave his successful business to the management of others and pursue training as a full-time pastor's assistant. That, in brief, is why Roy came to my office asking for pastoral advice about his future as a full-time servant of the Lord.

"Stephen," Roy didn't bother with formalities when he was anxious. "I've got a problem, a faith-shaking problem, and I have to talk with you ASAP." Whenever Roy says he has to talk with me as soon as possible, it usually means he is on a car phone two blocks from my office and will be walking in the door before I hang up the receiver. I wasn't far from wrong.

Over lunch Roy poured out his heart. "Pastor, I am really getting frustrated with my ministry training courses. I took these classes because I wanted to be better equipped to help our people when I visit them in the hospitals and nursing homes, but my profs keep wanting to teach me about the Maccabean period, the formation of the New Testament canon, and the communication of divine attributes to the person of Jesus Christ. I gotta tell you, I just don't see how that's gonna help me comfort people on their death beds!"

I couldn't help but smile as Roy told me of his frustration. I was secretly relieved that it wasn't a crisis of greater proportion. Roy detected my smile and responded.

"Don't laugh," he said. "Pastor Brassie has a doctorate and has been helping me with my homework, and he's making C's!" I could no longer contain myself and burst into a hearty laugh. Roy joined in, and it was some time before he could continue.

"You think it's funny," he finally said. "But you helped me with one assignment and I made a D on that one!" The humor of the moment helped relieve the tension and keep the issue in perspective.

"Do others in your class feel the way you do?" I asked.

"Well, I don't want to be critical," Roy said. "But I've been in the people business for a long time now, and the ones in the class who are getting good grades likely don't have a clue what it takes to talk with folks about real-life issues."

"Have you spoken to your professor about your feelings?" I asked.

"Yeah, I did. The last time we met I finally told him that I didn't see how my ability to explain the political tensions of the Intertestamental Period was going to help me comfort someone on their death bed."

"What did he say?" I had to ask.

"He said, you never know what you might be asked. What

would you do, Roy, if someone asked you something you didn't know?"

In typical Roy-like fashion he responded, "I would tell them, 'I don't know. We'll have to ask our pastor about that one—now let's talk about Jesus!' "

How Much Knowledge Is Enough?

Roy's story is funny, but it also has a serious side. How much do Christians need to know before they can begin to share their faith with those who know little or nothing about Jesus?

A famous British actor was being honored at a testimonial dinner by his friends and peers. As is the custom at such events, the time came when the guests began to gently clink their glasses while chanting, "Speech! Speech! Speech!" The actor rose to quiet the crowd and politely declined the invitation to make a speech. "I will however," he replied, "offer a recitation on the condition that my dear friend and lifelong pastor be permitted the same honor." His request was quickly granted.

He chose for his recitation the Twenty-third Psalm, and in dramatic and rich fashion he delivered the reading with eloquence. The audience responded with prolonged applause, both out of respect for his selection and the professional manner in which it was delivered.

Now came the moment when the actor's aged pastor was given the podium to make a similar offering. His body betrayed his years. In stooped posture he stood before them. The richness of his formerly strong voice had left him. There was no elocution in his delivery as he bowed his head and offered a quiet and personal recitation of the very same psalm. When he had finished, the crowd sat in hushed silence. The kind of silence that comes from deep personal reflection.

The guest of honor rose to help his beloved pastor back to his chair. Then, turning to his guests, he said, "The difference between these two renditions, in my humble opinion is that I, for my part, know the psalm. But this dear friend of mine—he quite obviously knows the Shepherd."

He knew the Shepherd and it was evident to all.

As Christians we each know the Shepherd and that knowledge is the difference between an eternity in heaven or an eternity in hell.

How soon should we begin to share our faith? How much should we know before we know enough to be an effective witness for our Savior? The Bible says, "How, then, can they call on the one they have not believed in? And how can they believe in the one of whom they have not heard? And how can they hear without someone preaching to them? And how can they preach unless they are sent? As it is written, 'How beautiful are the feet of those who bring good news! … faith comes from hearing the message, and the message is heard through the word of Christ' " (Romans 10:14–15, 17).

Sharing What You Know

The shepherds who visited the manger the night of Jesus' birth would have been hard pressed to explain the Incarnation (God taking flesh), but that did not stop them from, "glorifying and praising God for all that they had heard and seen, which were just as they had been told" (Luke 2:20).

The blind man healed by Jesus could not answer by what power he had been granted sight. In a simple but powerful way he said, "He put mud on my eyes, and I washed and now I see." When pressed to deny Christ and acknowledge the Lord as a common sinner, the simple witness of this blind man only gained greater strength. In words that have echoed through the centuries, he told the simple truth in simple fashion, "Whether He is a sinner or not, I don't know. One thing I do know. I was blind but now I see!" (John 9:25). He shared only what he knew, and for refusing to reject Christ was himself banned from the temple. Jesus, hearing of his plight, sought this simple believer and revealed Himself more fully to him.

You Don't Need to Be an Expert

A young boy was urged by his mother to apply for an after-school job at a neighborhood grocery. He made the appointment and appeared as scheduled for an interview with the store owner. The job was only stocking shelves and cleaning floors, but in the end, all business is "people business," so the owner asked the young man how he would handle an irate customer. The boy thought for a moment and then responded, "I would handle an irate customer the same way I'd handle the customer before them and the customer after them." The owner was pleased and hired the boy on the spot.

When he arrived home, the boy was eagerly greeted by his mother, who wanted to know how the interview had gone. "Super," replied her son. "The owner seemed impressed, and I got the job! By the way, Mom, what does *irate* mean?"

It isn't necessary to know all the answers before you begin to witness for the Lord. Share what you know and like Paul witness to the difference Christ has made in your life (see Acts 22:1–22 and Acts 26).

Growing as a Knowledgeable Christian

Please do not misunderstand. By no means should this discussion be mistaken as an argument against continued learning and a lifelong commitment to grow in the knowledge of salvation. The Bible argues just the opposite! "Like newborn babies, crave pure spiritual milk, so that by it you may grow up in your salvation, now that you have tasted that the Lord is good" (1 Peter 2:2–3). The apostle Paul urged the same growth commitment when he chided the Corinthians for their lack of maturity. "I could not address you as spiritual but as worldly—mere infants in Christ. I gave you milk, not solid food, for you were not yet ready for it. Indeed, you are still not ready. You are still worldly!" (1 Corinthians 3:1–3).

In the book of Hebrews the Lord repeats the admonition, "Therefore let us leave the elementary teachings about Christ and go on to maturity, not laying again the foundation of repentance from acts that lead to death, and of faith in God, instructions about baptisms, the laying on of hands, the resurrection of the dead, and eternal judgment. And God permitting, we will do so" (6:1–3). That which is healthy grows. Christians born by the power of God's Spirit desire to continue to grow in their faith and understanding of Him as long as they live. It is a never-ending need, but Christians should never use their lack of knowledge about the mature teachings of Scripture as a reason to excuse their unwillingness to witness.

Too many, far too many, Christians fail to act on the urging of Christ to speak of Him as a natural expression of faith in their daily life. We practice the posture of the hesitant whose motto is "Ready! aim … aim … aim … aim … aim." How much better the motto of the French Foreign Legion in their battle against earthly enemies: No Regrets! Their expanded theme is equally forceful, "If I fall—push me. If I stumble—pick me up. If I retreat—shoot me." As Paul told the first-century Christians, we too are in a battle. A battle for something more precious than earthly freedom or even life itself.

> For our struggle is not against flesh and blood, but against the rulers, against the authorities, against the powers of this dark world and against the spiritual forces of evil in the heavenly realms. Therefore put on the full armor of God, so that when the day of evil comes, you may be able to stand your ground, and after you have done everything, to stand. (Ephesians 6:12-13)

The Way of the Lord

The hesitancy to witness often comes from a sincere and honest humility on the part of Christians who feel unworthy to speak on behalf of the Lord. That is both a proper and an improper attitude at the same time. Proper, in the sense that apart from Christ we can do nothing. Improper, in that Christians can do all things through Christ who strengthens them. Once, when our congregation was considering a sizable commitment, a member expressed the opinion that "The Lord can pay for what He orders." In other words, if God asks us to do something, you can count on His necessary support to accomplish it. There is no question that the Lord has asked us to be His witnesses, even to the ends of the earth.

One of the guiding principles of service in the kingdom of the Lord is that God often recruits those of little or no status. When the task is eventually accomplished everyone will readily admit, "It must have been God!" This principle is demonstrated repeatedly in the lives of great biblical leaders.

- Abraham was old when God asked him to leave Ur.
- Moses was inarticulate. [Perhaps even stuttered.]
- Samuel was only a boy.
- King Saul was painfully shy.
- David was only a shepherd.
- Matthew was a tax collector.
- Peter was a simple fisherman.

As the Bible says, "We have this treasure in jars of clay to show that this all-surpassing power is from God and not from us" (2 Corinthians 4:7).

A Lesson from the Past

My favorite study of this principle at work is an examination of the book of Judges, and specifically the life of Gideon. Gideon is proof that God uses those who think little of themselves to accomplish His best work. Gideon is also proof that God has a sense of humor.

His remarkable story is told in Judges 6–8.

The time of Gideon's life was a period of oppression in Israel. The Midianites were so strong that many Israelites had fled to the mountains and were living in caves just to escape from their enemy. What few crops they were able to cultivate the Midianites stole. This is the setting for the story of Gideon.

The Bible tells us, "Gideon was threshing wheat in a winepress to keep it from the Midianites. When the angel of the Lord appeared to Gideon, he said, 'The LORD is with you, mighty warrior!' " (Judges 6:11–12).

Several things about this verse strike me immediately. First, Gideon could hardly be called *mighty* or a *warrior.* A wine press was logically located close to the vineyards, which were cultivated on the hills far from the fields where wheat was grown. At great inconvenience Gideon had hauled his wheat crop a great distance so he could escape any confrontation with the Midianites. The Lord saw something in Gideon that Gideon did not see in himself. The Lord called him a valiant warrior. Gideon shows by his response that the unusual nature of this greeting did not go unnoticed.

" 'But sir,' Gideon replied, 'if the LORD is with us, why has all this happened to us? Where are all His wonders that our fathers told us about when they said, "Did not the LORD bring us up out of Egypt?" But now the LORD has abandoned us and put us into the hand of Midian' " (Judges 6:13). There is deep-seated bitterness and cynicism in the response of Gideon. If he had any faith left at all, it has been stretched to the point of tearing. It would take the patience of the Lord and some watering of fleece before Gideon was ready to trust and believe. Gideon was immersed in his pain and the suffering of his people. He laid the blame fully on the Lord who, in his opinion, had abandoned Israel.

The Lord was gracious in His treatment of Gideon. He did not strike him dead for his insolence. He did not set his wheat on fire, nor even defensively explain how Israel's own disobedience had brought this trouble upon the land. No. Instead the Lord continued His positive assessment of Gideon and reiterated the opportunity before him. The Lord tells him, "Go in the strength you have and save Israel out of Midian's hand. Am I not sending you?" (Judges 6:14).

"In the strength you have"? What strength? The Lord challenged Gideon to quit feeling sorry for himself and tackle the impossible task of removing Midian's dominance. How could Gideon possibly succeed? Israel was cowering in caves! The Midianites had controlled the land for seven years—very likely Gideon could not even remember a period of national freedom. The Midianites by contrast were powerful, prosperous, and too numerous to count. How could Gideon possibly succeed? "Am I not sending you?" God asked. The promise of the Lord was Gideon's only hope.

Gideon remained unconvinced. Perhaps the Lord didn't know who he was dealing with! Gideon explained in detail his personal status in verse 15. "But Lord … how can I save Israel? My clan is the weakest in Manasseh, and I am the least in my family!" Genealogically speaking, Gideon was the bottom of the Israelite barrel.

You have to know some basic Old Testament history to understand Gideon's low opinion of himself. There were 12 sons of Jacob, which made up the 12 tribes of Israel. Because the Levites were not given land (as priests they were scattered among all the tribes) there remained only 11 land-holding tribes. Neither was Joseph given land but instead his two sons, Manasseh and Ephraim were each granted tribal status—one received Joseph's portion, and the other the portion of the Levites. Technically, neither Manasseh nor Ephraim were tribes of the same status as the rest. Manasseh was the oldest of Joseph's sons, and when Joseph brought his two boys to Jacob to receive the patriarch's blessing he presented Manasseh in his left hand (on his father's right side as he faced him) so that Manasseh might receive the greater blessing. Incredibly however, Jacob, although blinded by age, crossed his arms (against Joseph's vehement objections) and granted the greater blessing to the younger son Ephraim! *Gideon was therefore the youngest son of the least important family in the least important tribe of all of Israel!* He was the most unqualified man God could choose to lead the campaign against Midian. No one knew this fact better than Gideon.

God Often Prefers to Work through *"Simple" Christians*

Are you only a "simple Christian", not really qualified to be a witness for the Lord? The lesson of Gideon and the historic practice of God revealed in Scripture proves "God can pay for what God orders." If in His wisdom, the Lord chooses the person who appears the least qualified to do a great job, He is working true to form. The principle of the least is universally taught in the Bible. In his introductory comments to the Church at Corinth Paul invited the Christians there to take a hard look at themselves.

> Brothers, think of what you were when you were called. Not many of you were wise by human standards; not many were influential; not many were of noble birth. But God chose the foolish things of the world to shame the wise; God chose the weak things of the world to shame the strong. He chose the lowly things of this world and the despised things—and the things that are not—to nullify the things that are, so that no one may boast before Him. (1 Corinthians 1:26-29)

"If you want to boast about something," Paul reminds the church, "Boast about the Lord." It is not *what you know* nor *who you are* that matters in the kingdom of God. *It is who you know* that makes all the difference. You know the Shepherd ... and more important, the Shepherd knows you.

For Discussion

1. The author asks, "When do you know enough to tell other people about the Lord? How much do you have to know before you are able to be His witness?" How would you answer those questions?

2. Do you agree or disagree with the statement "Most Christians are educated far beyond their level of obedience"? Explain

your answer and suggest ways in which better balance can be obtained.

3. What are some lessons Christians can learn from a study of great leaders like Gideon? Is there an impossible job that is presenting itself to you or to your congregation that lacks the necessary leadership? How might Gideon's story bring comfort and hope?

4. What did Paul mean when he said, "I will not boast about myself, except about my weaknesses ... I will boast all the more gladly about my weaknesses, so that Christ's power may rest on me. That is why, for Christ's sake, I delight in weaknesses, in insults, in hardships, in persecutions, in difficulties. For when I am weak, then I am strong" (2 Corinthians 12:5, 9, 10)? How did Paul use his weaknesses—as an excuse or as a means of accomplishment?

5. When Paul described the congregation at Corinth, he said not many were wise by human standards, not many were influential, nor of privileged birth. Does that description still fit most congregations? Is there a reason why the wise, the influential, and those of privileged birth are not readily found in a Christian fellowship? How much does God desire to save them?

Session 2 No Contest— Wielding the Sword

One of the most unusual monuments to those who died in battle during World War II is found in Bly, Oregon. It should not surprise anyone that Bly, Oregon, would have a World War II memorial. Almost every town in the nation has a monument honoring the memory of those who made the ultimate sacrifice for their country. But this monument is different. It reads

> **THE ONLY PLACE**
> **ON THE AMERICAN CONTINENT**
> **WHERE DEATH RESULTED**
> **FROM ENEMY ACTION**
> **DURING WORLD WAR II**

What enemy action took place in Bly, Oregon?

The answer to that question lies buried in history, to events that began on a bright sunny day, April 18, 1942. That morning 16 B-25 bombers lifted off the deck of the aircraft carrier *Hornet*. Despite the brightness of the day, the low-flying bombers entered Japanese airspace undetected. The element of surprise was on their side. The Japanese had absolute confidence in the strength of their military, which they believed was in complete control of the Pacific war. The *Hornet* was cruising several hundred miles off the coast of Japan, believed to be preoccupied patrolling enemy shipping lanes.

We can only imagine the shock of the unsuspecting nation as the cities of Kobe, Nagoya, Osaka, and Tokyo, were rocked by the incendiary bombs of the U.S. aircraft. All the planes reached their targets and dropped their bombs.

The damage inflicted by Doolittle's raid was not the greatest accomplishment of the mission. In fact, the raid inflicted very little physical damage. The greatest accomplishment was the psychological impact on the Japanese people. Their homeland would never again be considered invulnerable. The April 18 bombing had changed the nature of the Pacific war, and the Japanese high command ordered a retaliatory strike over American soil. Project "Fu-Go" was implemented.

Since the early 1930s Japanese meteorologists had been aware of the strong winter jet stream that passed over Japan at speeds as great as 200 knots. Their military scientists conceived the idea of floating bomb-laden, hydrogen-filled balloons into those wind currents, which would carry their deadly payload over northwest portions of the United States.

The Japanese scientists devised an ingenious ballast-release system, controlled by an altimeter, which was powered by a small 2.3 volt battery. In the warmth of the sun the balloon would rise into the jet stream at altitudes as high as 38,000 feet. But at night, when temperatures at that altitude dropped as low as minus 50 degrees centigrade, the gas would contract and the balloon would descend as low as 3,000 feet. The battery-run altimeter would then trip a mechanism designed to release ballast in the form of sandbags until a minimum preset altitude was achieved. The falling and rising of the balloon during the 60 hours required to cross the ocean would bring the cargo of bombs over North America as the last "ballast" to be released on the forests and cities of the northwest.

The Japanese hoped their balloons would have the same effect on America that Doolittle's raid had on the people of Japan. The first balloon was released on Nov. 3, 1944, and by January 1945 sightings over the Pacific Northwest had became routine. For some time the purpose and nature of the balloons remained a mystery. Americans speculated they were runaway Japanese weather balloons, or parts of wayward antiaircraft defenses. But unexplained explosions and fireballs in the sky were also being reported from California to Oregon. (The balloons were rigged to self-destruct after dropping their deadly payload.) It was not until a U.S. pilot shot one of the balloons down over Alturas, California, that the exact nature of the plan was discovered.

But the ingenious scheme to set the thick forests and cities of the United States ablaze never materialized. The only time the jet stream was strong enough to accomplish its delivery was when the northwest was snowpacked and frozen, its least flammable time.

Project "Fu-Go" was not a total failure. On May 6, 1945, one of the "Fu-Go" balloons floated to the ground in Bly, Oregon. Elsie Mitchell and five nearby children were intrigued. As they stooped to investigate the curiosity, one of the bombs exploded, killing all six people.

Because news blackouts were honored by American newspapers, the Japanese never knew if project "Fu-Go" had succeeded or failed. American bombing of mainland Japan intensified, resulting in the destruction of the factories producing the balloons and the hydrogen needed to float them. After only five months, the Japanese abandoned the "Fu-Go" project.

On Aug. 6, 1945, at 2:10 A.M., a B-29 named the *Enola Gay* took off from Tinian in the Marianas Islands. At 9:30 A.M., the first atomic bomb fell on Hiroshima. One bomb killed 92,233 people immediately and injured another 37,425. But the proud nation of Japan refused to surrender.

On Aug. 9, 1945, Major Charles Sweeney flew a second B-29 over the city of Nagasaki. The bomb dropped that day killed 23,753 people and injured 43,020 more, many of whom would not recover. The next day, Aug. 10, 1945, Japan surrendered under the provision that its emperor be allowed to maintain his sovereign-ruler status.

It Was No Contest

How do you compare balloons controlled by 2.3 volt batteries to B-29 bombers armed with atomic bombs, project "Fu-Go" to The Manhattan Project. *It was no contest.* The atomic bombs leveled their targets, detonating with a force equivalent to 20,000 tons of TNT. As far as we know, Elsie Mitchell and the five children of Bly, Oregon, were the only casualties of operation "Fu-Go." Nearly 150,000 Japanese died compared to 6 Americans in Bly. Although thousands of the deadly balloons were released, only 350 were ever confirmed over American soil.

The Greatest Power Known to Man

Balloons were no match to a self-sustained atomic reaction. Neither can any Christian, wielding the Sword of the Lord (which is the Word of God—Hebrews 4:12, Ephesians 6:17), be defeated in their battle against the devil, the world, or the temptation of their own sinful nature. God's Word is power in print. And His power is unmatched by anything the enemy has at his disposal. It is no contest.

When Christians are asked, "By what power does God do this or that?" The biblical answer is always, "By the power of God's Spirit, who works through Scripture." The word for "power" in the Greek New Testament is *dunamis*. It is the very same word we use for the explosive substance called dynamite. God's Word is dynamite! Paul described it as the Christian's offensive weapon "against the spiritual forces of evil in heavenly realms" (Ephesians 6:12). As the "Sword of the Spirit," God's Word packs the power Christians need to overcome the enemies of faith. As Luther's famous hymn puts it:

> **Though devils all the world should fill,**
> **All eager to devour us,**
> **We tremble not, we fear no ill,**
> **They shall not overpower us.**
> **This world's prince may still**
> **Scowl fierce as he will,**
> **He can harm us none,**
> **He's judged; the deed is done;**
> **One little word can fell him!**

Not just any word can fell Satan. The Word of God invoked by faith is the Word that fells him. Luke tells a story about nonbelievers who were using Jesus' name as a magic charm in an attempt to cast out demons for fame and fortune. They learned a hard lesson about conducting spiritual warfare without the power of God's Word.

> Some Jews who went around driving out evil spirits tried to invoke the name of the Lord Jesus over those who were demon-possessed. They would say, "In the name of Jesus, whom Paul preaches, I command you to come out." Seven sons of Sceva, a Jewish chief priest, were doing this. One day the evil spirit answered them, "Jesus I know, and I know about Paul, but who are you?" Then the man who had the evil spirit jumped on them and overpowered them all. He gave them such a beating that they ran out of the house naked and bleeding. (Acts 19:13–16)

The Bible says, "Without faith it is impossible to please God, because anyone who comes to Him must believe that He exists and that He rewards those who earnestly seek Him" (Hebrews 11:6). Likewise, faith is the key to unleashing the power of God's Word in our Christian life and witness.

Unsheathing the Sword of the Lord

Christians are warned to not be like the Israelites of the Old Testament who had God's promise of assistance but lacked faith to trust

His Word. Our present situation is no different than theirs.

> Since the promise of entering his rest still stands, let us be careful that none of you be found to have fallen short of it. For we also have had the Gospel preached to us, just as they did; but the message they heard was of no value to them, because those who heard did not combine it with faith. (Hebrews 4:1–2)

Consider the example of the Christian college student who enrolled in a course entitled "The Bible As Literature." She was disappointed when the professor made it clear that he was not a believer in the God of Scripture, but admired the book and believed its pages contained excellent examples of ancient poetry and prose. The Christian student challenged his thinking, saying that the Bible was more than good literature. "It was," she believed, "the power of God in print. A love letter from God to His children."

"For me," he insisted, "it is only literature."

"That" she replied, "is the way it always seems to those who read other people's mail."

The more things change, the more they remain the same! Paul told the Christians at Corinth, "For the message of the cross is foolishness to those who are perishing, but to us who are being saved it is the power of God. For it is written: 'I will destroy the wisdom of the wise; the intelligence of the intelligent I will frustrate'" (1 Corinthians 1:18–19).

Regardless of what people may think, the Bible is not unclear when it makes claims to power. Refusing to take credit for the faith of those in Corinth, Paul used his weakness and anxiety as a testimony to the power of God unleashed whenever the Gospel is proclaimed.

> When I came to you, brothers, I did not come with eloquence or superior wisdom as I proclaimed to you the testimony about God. For I resolved to know nothing while I was with you except Jesus Christ and Him crucified. I came to you in weakness and fear, and with much trembling. My message and my preaching were not with wise and persuasive words, but with a demonstration of the Spirit's power, so that your faith might not rest on men's wisdom, but on God's power. (1 Corinthians 2:1–5)

The Most Important Lesson of All

This may be the most important passage in all of Scripture concerning the nature of conversion and the means by which it is accomplished. Conversion does not rest on a Christian's ability to articulate an air-tight presentation. That is a no-win approach to witnessing, because when you win by argumentation you still lose. And when you lose by argumentation you also lose. As the old axiom correctly states, Those convinced against their will remain unconvinced. Conversion is God's business, not ours. It is done by the power of the Gospel, not by our ability to craft a convincing testimony. When Christians use His Word, God's power is brought to bear. It is the most we can do. It is all we can do. It is more than enough. From the beginning of time to the end of the world, God has and will continue to accomplish His will by the power of His word.

- By the power of His Word He created the heaven and earth (Hebrews 11:3).
- By the power of His Word nonbelievers come to faith (Romans 10:17).
- By the power of His Word simple water becomes life-giving Baptism (Acts 2:38–39).
- By the power of His Word under wine and bread Christians receive His body and blood, for the forgiveness of sins, life and salvation (Matthew 26:26–28).
- By the power of His Word the dead shall rise on judgment day (1 Thessalonians 4:16).

God's Word is His means of grace. It is the means by which He unleashes His power to change the hearts of the lost and strengthen the faith of the saved. Sharing the simple truth of salvation through Jesus is our part in the task.

Power in Practice—An Historic Example

Who would have thought a simple monk in the hinterlands of Germany would be used by God to initiate and sustain a movement that would shatter the military and spiritual dominance of a corrupted papacy? Martin Luther's position looked precarious. He had boldly stood before the emperor, his own elector, and the pope's emissary to acknowledge that his writings often disagreed with the official positions of the church. When asked if he would defend them all or recant any portions of his statements, the accused asked for and received permission to consider his answer.

The next day, on April 18, 421 years before Doolittle's famous raid on Japan, a different kind of bomb reigned down on a different kind of enemy.

After dividing his writings into three categories, Luther defended the first two stacks as representing the historic faith of the church, which none could deny. Concerning the third group he said,

> In these, I attacked certain persons whom I thought to be enemies of the Gospel. I admit that I may have used unkind language here and there. For this I apologize. But I can not take back what I said in defending God's truth. If I did, then sin and evil would increase their power. Show me from the Bible where I have taught falsely. If you can, then I will be the first to burn my books. Your majesty, I put myself in your hands. Please do not let my enemies make you angry at me without good reason.

The bomb had been dropped and the pride of the church had been challenged! The authorities determined that the upstart monk had not really answered the question. Luther was told to end his debate and give a simple answer—"Do you or do you not recant your books and the errors in them?" The retaliation was about to be unleashed. Luther's only defense was the power of God revealed in His word. It was enough—more than enough.

> Since your Majesty and your lordships want a simple, clear and true answer, I will give it, neither horned or toothed. Unless I am convinced by the teachings of Holy Scripture or by sound reasoning—for I do not believe either the pope or councils alone, since they have often made mistakes and have even said the exact opposite about the same point—I am bound by the Scriptures I have quoted and my conscience is held captive by the Word of God. I cannot and will not recant anything, for it is neither safe nor right to go against one's conscience. God help me. Here I stand. I can do no other! Amen.

God did help Luther withstand the slings and arrows of his day. He died of natural causes in the town of his birth in 1546, 25 years after his now-famous bombing run over the courts of the emperor in a place called Worms, Germany. He had tested and found the counsel of David to be as faithful in 1521 as in the day God inspired its writing,

> From heaven the LORD looks down
>   and sees all mankind;
> from His dwelling place He watches
>   all who live on earth—
> He who forms the hearts of all,
>   who considers everything they do.
> No king is saved by the size of his army;
>   no warrior escapes by his great strength.
> A horse is a vain hope for deliverance;
>   despite all its great strength it cannot save.
> But the eyes of the LORD are on those who fear Him,
>   on those whose hope is in His unfailing love,
>   to deliver them from death
>   and keep them alive in famine.
> We wait in hope for the LORD;
>   He is our help and our shield.
> In Him our hearts rejoice,
>   for we trust in His holy name. (Psalm 33:13–21)

The Bible teaches and Christians confess that "Jesus Christ is the same yesterday and today and forever" (Hebrews 13:8). The God who restored the Gospel to His church in 1521 is more than able to empower farmers, secretaries, engineers, lawyers, teachers—people from every walk of life—to speak with power in the neighborhoods and offices of America.

A Lesson from Scripture

One of my favorite Bible stories that shows the power of God in the life of a simple believer is found in 2 Kings 5. Elisha is pictured as a seasoned veteran with great confidence in the power of God. What a change from his days as the insecure understudy of Elijah who would permit no discussion of his master's eminent departure, leaving him to carry on the ministry of the Lord! But the story is not really about Elisha. It is a story about the power of a young girl's simple witness in the home of her enemy. It is a story about the power of God's Word.

We don't even know the young girl's name. She had been taken captive during a raid by the Arameans upon the northern tribes of Israel. Perhaps her parents had been killed. It is hard to imagine a father or mother not fighting to death out of love for their child. This history is not told us in the story. We are told that the girl had been trained as a servant to Naaman's wife. Naaman was in charge of his king's army, and he was a leper. Leprosy was the cancer of ancient times. Naaman's disease would continue to worsen until he would lose his position, his friends, his family, and eventually his life. The young girl who waited on Naaman's wife was old enough to know how desperate the situation was for Naaman and his family. She was also old enough when captured to know the difference between the true God of Israel and the gods of her enemy. With a love that only God can provide, this child expressed heartfelt concern for her master's welfare. "I wish," she told her mistress, "that my master were with the prophet who is in Samaria. Then he would cure him of his leprosy."

In childlike fashion this young girl gave a strong witness to the confidence she had in the God of her nation. She was confident her God's prophet could make a difference. Naaman, desperate for a cure, immediately acted on her advice and gained his king's permission to travel to visit the king of Israel.

What a contrast is shown between the young girl's confidence and king of Israel! When Naaman appeared before the king with gifts and a letter requesting his assistance, the king tore his clothes. He believed there was nothing that could be done for Naaman, and when it was discovered, war would surely follow.

But Elisha heard of Naaman's visit and sent word to the king saying, "Why have you torn your robes? Have the man come to me and he will know that there is a prophet in Israel." Notice that Elisha doesn't claim any personal authority or special power except as a prophet of God. The power is not his, it is in his office as a spokesman for God. The power is in God's Word, not in the healing touch of Elisha. To make this point especially clear, when Naaman came in all his pomp and glory, Elisha would not even go out to greet him! "What an insult!" Naaman must have thought. Elisha sent a messenger with powerful words of healing from God. What happens next is predictable.

> But Naaman went away angry and said, "I thought that he [Elisha] would surely come out to me and stand and call on the name of the LORD his God, wave his hand over the spot and cure

me of my leprosy. Are not Abana and Pharpar, the rivers of Damascus, better than any of the waters of Israel? Couldn't I wash in them and be cleansed? So he turned and went off in a rage. (2 Kings 5:11-12)

It is hard for proud people to be humble. It was not the water that would do the healing. It would be obedience to the Word of God. Notice that Elisha allows Naaman to leave angry. He doesn't try to convince him about the power of God's Word. The Word of God does its own fighting. He knew what another prophet wrote:

As the rain and the snow come down from heaven, and do not return to it without watering the earth and making it bud and flourish, so that it yields seed for the sower and bread for the eater, so is My word that goes out from My mouth: It will not return to Me empty, but will accomplish what I desire and achieve the purpose for which I sent it. (Isaiah 55:10-11)

After Naaman had time to reflect on his great need and God's great offer, he began to reconsider the counsel of the prophet. Simple servants were also used by God to advise their master, and he submitted to the Word of God. The result was twofold. As promised, he was cleansed of his disease. But more important, his heart was turned. "Now I know," he said, "that there is no God in all the world except in Israel." He also pledged to never again worship any god except the true God. All of this God accomplished by the simple but powerful witness of an obscure slave girl living in a foreign land.

No-Fault/No-Credit Witnessing

God's Word is power in print. This principle is a lesson every Christian must remember. When the truth of God's Word is shared simply and honestly, the Holy Spirit goes to work. Christians can take no credit for those who receive the Gospel and come to faith. Neither should they accept blame for those who don't.

When Jesus sent His disciples out on a mission of witness. He gave them a simple charge. To those who received the Gospel, the disciples were to say, "The Kingdom of God is near you." To those who rejected the Gospel, the disciples were to say, "The Kingdom of God is near" (Luke 10:9, 11).

Christians are inclined to take rejection of the Gospel personally, as though they have failed in making a proper witness to Jesus.

Such thoughts are based on the false belief that our witness, not the Holy Spirit working through God's Word creates faith. Remember—to keep this point clear (and because of his reputation) Elisha did not even personally appear before Naaman. Jesus reminded His disciples of this important lesson when He said, "He who listens to you listens to Me; he who rejects you rejects Me; but he who rejects Me rejects Him who sent Me" (Luke 10:16). Witnessing with power is about telling the simple truth as revealed by God in His Word. It does its own convincing.

Whose Job Is It Anyway?

Knowing the difference between letting God's truth go to work and working to convince people through our effort frees Christians from the fear of failure. Not everyone with whom we share the Gospel will believe. Not everyone who saw and heard Jesus believed either (John 6:66). As Isaiah said, "All day long I have held out my hands to an obstinate people, who walk in ways not good, pursuing their own imaginations" (Isaiah 65:2). People have and will continue to reject the Gospel, but it was also Isaiah who spoke the hopeful prophecy, "I revealed myself to those who did not ask for me; I was found by those who did not seek me. To a nation that did not call on my name, I said, 'Here am I, here am I'" (Isaiah 65:1).

For Discussion

1. According to the author, what is the most important lesson for Christians to remember on the issue of conversion? What biblical proof does the author offer as evidence?

2. Why was it so hard for Naaman to accept God's Word? Why do nonbelievers find it hard to accept God's truth today?

3. What common counsel did Paul give to the young pastors Timothy and Titus in 1 Timothy 6:20–21 and Titus 3:8–11? Why is this counsel still so important in the Christian church today?

4. What did the author mean when he said, "If you win you lose and if you lose, you lose?" Why is this an important concept?

5. Looking back on your own life of faith, how was the Word used to bring about your conversion? If through infant Baptism, locate a copy of Luther's Small Catechism and write down the answer to the question, "How can water do such great things?"

6. How has this study helped you better understand or clarify your task as a Christian witness? (Consider 1 Corinthians 4:1–5 for additional insight.)

Session 3 Know Your Enemy

Jesus once said, "Suppose a king is about to go to war against another king. Will he not first sit down and consider whether he is able with ten thousand men to oppose the one coming against him with twenty thousand?" (Luke 14:31). Jesus was cautioning those who might thoughtlessly accept His Lordship. In effect, He was saying, "Before you make a commitment, you should know what it requires." God does not want His people to be uninformed.

The mission is clear. Jesus spelled out His expectations in a conversation with His disciples on Easter evening. Luke recorded the discussion for our benefit in the last chapter of his gospel.

> **Then He opened their minds so they could understand the Scriptures. He told them, "This is what is written: The Christ will suffer and rise from the dead on the third day, and repentance and forgiveness of sins will be preached in His name to all nations, beginning at Jerusalem." (Luke 24:45–47)**

On the day of His ascension, Jesus reiterated His expectation. "Go and make disciples of all nations, baptizing them in the name of the Father and of the Son and of the Holy Spirit, and teaching them to obey everything I have commanded you" (Matthew 28:19–20). Christ's expectations are clear but our understanding of the opposition is purposely obscured by the master of deceit. If we are to "fight the good fight" of faith (1 Timothy 1:18) we would be wise to learn something about the enemy.

Learning the Hard Way

Two summers ago, two other fathers and I took our sons on a canoe trip into the boundary waters of Minnesota. We decided to venture into an area that was off the beaten path and guaranteed the best chance of seeing moose, eagles, beaver, and black bear. It was a section of the boundary waters that strictly forbid the use of motors. We would have to paddle the 50 miles in and out by sheer effort. There were 10 of us so we rounded up 5 canoes, strapped them to our cars and headed north.

For the most part, the trip fulfilled every expectation. Before we had paddled even a couple of miles we were taking pictures of long-legged moose grazing on vegetation from the bottom of the shallow lakes we paddled through. Eagles circled overhead and the beavers announced our arrival with tail-slapping explosions. The current was flowing in our direction so we made good time on the first day, except for the portages.

Portages are pathways around dangerous stretches of rapids, waterfalls, or obstructions on the river. Because the area was less traveled, so were the portages. The paths were narrow, winding, and overgrown, some as long as a mile. Whenever a degree of safety could be assured, we avoided the portage by "shooting the rapids," or by walking along the rocky shore, floating our canoes down the river with long ropes. It was not always easy to agree on the best procedure in a given situation. The boys thought it crazy to carry anything when a fast ride could do the job for them.

Our maps and guidebooks were of some help, but the water levels fluctuated so much their value was limited. Since none of us had been on this river before, whenever possible we walked along the length of the rapids before making our decision. We were doing well until we came to the longest portage of the trip.

The monster portage was a direct route through difficult terrain to save as many pack-laden steps as possible. The river, on the other hand, twisted, turned and dropped a dozen different ways before entering the lake below. We couldn't afford to risk our gear without a good look at the danger, and deep ravines and sharp turns made observation of the entire rapids impossible. We decided to carry our gear through the mosquito-infested forest and see how the white water looked from the other end. After a couple of trips, we agreed to shoot the rapids with empty canoes to save the trouble of carrying them such a long distance. Our most experienced canoeists went first, while the rest awaited the outcome and to receive any suggestions the first crew might offer about the best route. After strapping on their life vests and pushing out into the fast water, the first canoe disappeared quickly around the first turn.

It was quite a ride, and a good deal faster than walking the mile up and down the slippery rocks! They were soaked and their canoe was a third full of water, but otherwise all went well. They reported a few nasty turns and a couple of foaming drops but nothing so serious as to make the trip unsafe. "The trick," they reminded the rest, "was keeping the canoe straight in the fast water."

Encouraged by the first team's success, two 17-year-olds were the next to try. At that age most young boys "walk 10 feet tall and bullet-proof"—our sons were no exception. They were confident they could do anything a 40-year-old could do, and probably better. The rest of the party positioned themselves along the sheer walls of the river like spectators at an Olympic bobsled competition. Everyone waited to cheer their final turn and entrance into the last stretch of white water before entering the lake below. The cheers turned to laughter as a paddle rounded the bend followed closely by two teenagers shooting feet-first down through the foam. Their swamped canoe made the turn behind them and began rolling in the turbulence. Unfortunately it hung up on boulders in the middle of the stream and by sheer force was plunged to the bottom. Everyone made a valiant effort to retrieve the "sub" but to no avail. The force of the water was so great we were unable to roll, drag, or otherwise free it from its watery grave. If it hasn't broken apart or been freed by passersby during low water, it is still lodged there, and like all creation is now groaning to be set free at the coming of the Lord! (Romans 8:21–22).

After recovering from the hypothermia of our salvage attempt, we went forth a canoe lighter and a little wiser. We were thankful no one had been hurt and no gear had been lost. In the often unforgiving world of nature, lack of experience can be costly, even life-threatening. Our misfortune on the river cost each family $150— the price of a borrowed canoe. In the matter of spiritual combat the costs are much greater. They are of eternal consequence. Lives will be lost forever in hell if we underestimate or miscalculate the schemes of the enemy.

No Place for Trial and Error

There are always two ways to learn anything. We can learn by our mistakes, or we can take the wise counsel of experts and avoid the pitfalls of the uninformed. Christians can't afford risking souls through a trial-and-error course in spiritual warfare. It is a disastrous and needless exercise in futility. Paul reminded the Christians at Ephesus that war with Satan is never a fair fight. Without significant help from the Lord, the enemy has all the advantages.

> Our struggle is not against flesh and blood, but against the rulers, against the authorities, against the powers of this dark world and against the spiritual forces of evil in the heavenly realms. Therefore put on the full armor of God, so that when the day of evil comes, you may be able to stand your ground, and after you have done everything, to stand. (Ephesians 6:12-13)

God's Word is not silent on the subject of our enemy. Informed by trustworthy intelligence, we stand not only a good chance against the superior power of the enemy, we are guaranteed victory. This chapter is designed to better inform those God has called to wage the war under the direction of Christ our King. I like the way David described the advantage of the well-informed in Psalm 119.

> Your commands make me wiser than my enemies,
> for they are ever with me.
> I have more insight than all my teachers,
> for I meditate on Your statutes.
> I have more understanding than the elders,
> for I obey Your precepts.
> I have kept my feet from every evil path
> so that I might obey Your word. (119:98-101)

As we studied in the previous session, God's Word is power in-print. David found it better than good advice, less painful than experience, and more wise than the counsel of the wisest teacher or most experienced veteran. God has revealed to us the secrets of the enemy so he can be avoided, neutralized, and defeated.

In his explanation to the Sixth Petition of the Lord's Prayer, Martin Luther made it clear exactly who the enemy is and how he works. He wrote,

> We pray in this petition that God would guard and keep us so that the devil, the world, and our sinful nature may not deceive us or mislead us into false belief, despair, and other great shame and vice. Although we are attacked by these things, we pray that we may finally overcome them and win the victory.

Avoiding Costly Mistakes

There are two mistakes Christians frequently make when engaging in spiritual warfare. First, they fail to take Satan and his tactics seriously enough. Others, on the other hand, treat him as God's equal, which he is not. Using God's Word, let's take a look at the great deceiver and prepare ourselves to attack on the front where he is most threatened and most vulnerable—the campaign to rescue the souls of the lost.

Knowing the Enemy

Satan is a fallen angel, nothing more but nothing less. He was created by God and is therefore not God's equal. He has none of God's divine attributes. Students of the Scripture would say, "It means he has none of the omni gifts!" (*Omni* is a Latin term meaning "all.") He is not omniscient (all-knowing), omnipresent (everywhere at once), omnipotent (all powerful), neither is he fair, unchangeable, gracious, or just. He was not created evil, for the Bible clearly teaches, "God saw all that He had made, and it was very good" (Genesis 1:31). The Bible tells us about the devil's downfall.

> There was war in heaven. Michael and his angels fought against the dragon, and the dragon and his angels fought back. But he was not strong enough, and they lost their place in heaven. The great dragon was hurled down—that ancient serpent called the devil, or Satan, who leads the whole world astray. He was hurled to the earth, and his angels with him. Then I heard a loud voice in heaven say: "Now have come the salvation and the power and the kingdom of our God, and the authority of His Christ. For the accuser of our brothers, who accuses them before our God day and night, has been hurled down. They overcame him by the blood of the Lamb and by the word of their testimony; they did not love their lives so much as to shrink from death. Therefore rejoice, you heavens and you who dwell in them! But woe to the earth and the sea, because the devil has gone down to you! He is filled with fury, because he knows that his time is short." (Revelation 12:7–12)

He Lies and Is the Father of Lies

Notice that Satan is called "the accuser of our brothers." It is unclear whether this is a reference to accusations made against the first family on earth or against his fellow angels. What is not unclear is the nature of his sin. Jesus once described those who opposed Him saying, "You belong to your father, the devil, and you want to

carry out your father's desire. He was a murderer from the beginning, not holding to the truth, for there is no truth in him. When
he lies, he speaks his native language, for he is a liar and the father
of lies" (John 8:44).

We can expect those under the influence of Satan to play fast
and free with the truth. As disciples of their master they will naturally engage in distortion of the truth. Dr. Sam Nafzger, the executive director of the Commission on Theology and Church Relations
for The Lutheran Church-Missouri Synod, says, "I used to believe
that heresy was simply falsehood taught as truth. Now I believe
that heresy appears most often as truth removed from its necessary
context in the whole counsel of God." Satan is sly. He uses only bits
and pieces of God's truth out of context to confuse and misguide
His followers and their opponents. Remember how the devil quoted
the Scriptures out of context in his vain attempt to lure Jesus into
sin? (See Luke 4:9ff.) Paul said the twisting of truth by false teachers should not surprise Christians.

> Such men are false apostles, deceitful workmen,
> masquerading as apostles of Christ. And no wonder, for Satan
> himself masquerades as an angel of light. It is not surprising,
> then, if his servants masquerade as servants of righteousness.
> Their end will be what their actions deserve. (2 Corinthians
> 11:13–15)

The first alert for Christians engaged in spiritual warfare is a
"truth alert." When others oppose God's Word, be careful to listen
completely to what is said and ask clarifying questions. If possible,
ask for explanations in printed form so that like the Berean Christians you might be considered of more noble character than the
Thessalonians, because "they received the message with great
eagerness and examined the Scriptures every day to see if what Paul
said was true" (Acts 17:11).

Behavior Is a Window to the Heart

Jesus also said you can know a tree by its fruit. "Do people
pick grapes from thorn bushes, or figs from thistles? Likewise
every good tree bears good fruit, but a bad tree bears bad fruit. A
good tree cannot bear bad fruit, and a bad tree cannot bear good
fruit. Every tree that does not bear good fruit is cut down and

thrown into the fire. Thus, by their fruit you will recognize them" (Matthew 7:16–20). Study the "deeds of flesh" as recorded in Galatians 5.

> The acts of the sinful nature are obvious: sexual immorality, impurity and debauchery; idolatry and witchcraft; hatred, discord, jealousy, fits of rage, selfish ambition, dissensions, factions and envy; drunkenness, orgies, and the like. I warn you, as I did before, that those who live like this will not inherit the kingdom of God. (Galatians 5:19-21)

The second alert is a "behavior alert." Behaviors that are persistently and unashamedly contrary to the Word of God identify those who are living outside the saving grace of Jesus. Remember, the purpose in such identification is not to pass judgment; for judgment of the lost will come in God's way and in God's time, not ours. Jesus said, "God did not send His Son into the world to condemn the world, but to save the world through Him" (John 3:17).

The natural tendency of Christians to become frustrated with evil and those who perpetuate it is understandable. By all means and in every way we must oppose evil and stand for truth. But at the same time we must separate our disgust for evil from those Satan uses to promote his deceit. We will have little influence for good if, like Pharisees, we are condescending and judgmental of others. The lost, knowingly or not, are under the control of Satan and are only being true to their nature. Despite their best efforts and personal commitment (no matter how concerted), they remain unable to overcome and obtain the victory. (Remember: the fight is not one of equals.) Paul clarified this point for the Christians at Corinth.

> I have written you in my letter not to associate with sexually immoral people—not at all meaning the people of this world who are immoral, or the greedy and swindlers, or idolaters. In that case you would have to leave this world. But now I am writing you that you must not associate with anyone who calls himself a brother but is sexually immoral or greedy, an idolater or a slanderer, a drunkard or a swindler. With such a man do not even eat. What business is it of mine to judge those outside the church? (1 Corinthians 5:9-12)

The steps of church discipline as described in Matthew 18 are for the restoration of believers, not as a guide to rescuing the lost.

The apostle told the Christians of Ephesus to remember that, "There but for the grace of God, go I!" He put it in different words.

> All of us also lived among them at one time, gratifying the cravings of our sinful nature and following its desires and thoughts. Like the rest, we were by nature objects of wrath. But because of His great love for us, God, who is rich in mercy, made us alive with Christ even when we were dead in transgressions—it is by grace you have been saved. (Ephesians 2:3-5)

Seeing the Lost as Victims

The third and last alert we will discuss in this session is hurt. Satan is an evil master. Because of his nature, he is unwilling to allow even those within his control to enjoy the benefits of his power.

The Rev. Philip Lochhaas, the former executive director of The Lutheran Church-Missouri Synod's Commission on Organizations tells the story of a pastor who was asked to officiate at the funeral of a young man who had committed suicide. Before shooting himself he wrote, "I made a pact with Satan to serve him if he made me popular, but now he owns my mind and I can't stand it anymore."

Those living out of fellowship with God are living lives apart from the one they were created to enjoy. As a young boy growing up in a rural church in Indiana, I still remember the words our pastor recited as he prepared God's people for the celebration of the Lord's Supper. Holy Communion is a wonderful Sacrament that offers forgiveness of sins and solidifies our union with God through the body and blood of our Lord Jesus Christ. It is the way God intended for us to live in fellowship with Him before the Fall.

To prepare us for participating in the Sacrament the pastor would sometimes read "The Exhortation" from "The Order of the Confessional Service" in *The Lutheran Hymnal*.

> Dearly beloved: Forasmuch as we purpose to come to the Holy Supper of our Lord Jesus Christ, it becometh us diligently to examine ourselves, as St. Paul exhorteth us. For this holy Sacrament hath been instituted for the special comfort and strengthening of those who humbly confess their sins and hunger and thirst after righteousness.

But if we thus examine ourselves, we shall find nothing in us but sin and death, from which we can in no wise set ourselves free. Therefore our Lord Jesus Christ hath had mercy upon us and hath taken upon Himself our nature, that so He might fulfill for us the whole will and Law of God and for us and for our deliverance suffer death and all that we by our sins have deserved.

Did you notice the phrase *But if we thus examine ourselves, we shall find nothing in us but sin and death, from which we can in no wise set ourselves free*. This is the condition of those who are lost and under Satan's control. Roger Staubach described this condition in a poem he recited during his speech at the "Success 1994" conference in Dallas, Tex.

The Cold Within

Six humans trapped by happenstance, in bleak and bitter cold.
Each one possessed a stick of wood, or so the story's told.
Their dying fire in need of logs, the first man held his back;
For of the faces round the fire, he noticed one was black.
The next man looking cross the way, saw one not of his church,
And couldn't bring himself to give the fire his stick of birch.
The third one sat in tattered clothes, he gave his coat a hitch.
Why should his log be put to use to warm the idle rich?
The rich man just sat back and thought of the wealth he had in store,
And how to keep what he had earned from the lazy, shiftless, poor.
The black man's face bespoke revenge as the fires passed from his sight.
For all he saw in his stick of wood was chance to spite the white.
The last man of this forlorn group did naught except for gain.
Giving only to those who gave was how he played the game.
Their logs held tight in death's still hand was proof of human sin,
They didn't die from the cold without—they died from the cold within.

(Roger Staubach's speech was delivered during his March 31 presentation at the "Success 1994" conference in Dallas, Tex. The poem *The Cold Within* was attributed by Staubach to James Patrick Kenny, an Indianapolis high school student.)

Christians need to see past the evil perpetuated by those who are lost and recognize the source of their evil. See their hurt. They are dying from the cold within. Unfortunately the hurting are inclined to spread their hurt around—inflicting pain, suffering, and destruction in their wake. Our task is to accomplish their rescue armed with the Word of God and accompanied by the ever-present power of the Holy Spirit.

The Victory Is Ours

As Christians committed to the cause of Christ and the rescue of those in the grasp of Satan, we need to recognize the limits of Satan's power and affirm the unlimited power of God. The writings of the evangelist John have been described as waters so gentle that a mouse might wade, and so deep that an elephant might drown. In his simple but powerful way he has written,

> This is how you can recognize the Spirit of God: Every spirit that acknowledges that Jesus Christ has come in the flesh is from God, but every spirit that does not acknowledge Jesus is not from God. This is the spirit of the antichrist, which you have heard is coming and even now is already in the world. You, dear children, are from God and have overcome them, because the one who is in you is greater than the one who is in the world. (1 John 4:2-4)

The One who is in us is greater than the one who is in the world. We cannot eliminate the frustrating interference of Satan in our life's witness anymore than Paul, who was once frustrated by Satan in his attempt to visit the Christians at Thessalonica (see 1 Thessalonians 2:18). But at the same time, neither will we grant him more respect than he merits as a defeated enemy of the cross. James provided a simple formula for waging the war with this unseen enemy. "Submit yourselves, then, to God. Resist the devil, and he will flee from you" (James 4:7). Carefully notice the order: (1) Submit to God. (2) In His strength resist the devil. (3) He will flee from you.

You cannot stand unarmed before an unseen enemy as mighty as a fallen angel, but he cannot stand long before a soldier of the cross armed with the Sword of the Spirit, which is the Word of God (Ephesians 6:17).

How do we draw near to God? Anticipating our question, James provided the answer. "Come near to God and He will come near to you. Wash your hands, you sinners, and purify your hearts, you doubters. Grieve, mourn and wail. Change your laughter to mourning and your joy to gloom. Humble yourselves before the Lord, and He will lift you up" (James 4:8–10).

We draw near to God through humble confession of our sins. In Christ we receive our acceptance. It is this very truth that gave Paul the courage he possessed as a witness for Christ until his death by execution. Because the victory was already his, he did not shrink from a life of bold and courageous witness despite the threats, mistreatment, and frequent imprisonments. He dared to be different and knew his efforts, enabled by the Word and the power of the Spirit, would find success on the spiritual battleground of life.

> Thanks be to God! He gives us the victory through our Lord Jesus Christ. Therefore, my dear brothers, stand firm. Let nothing move you. Always give yourselves fully to the work of the Lord, because you know that your labor in the Lord is not in vain. (1 Corinthians 15:57-58)

For Discussion

1. Name some of Satan's tactics that have kept or hindered Christians from waging successful rescue campaigns for lost souls? (How has he been able to keep you from participating more fully in the battle?)

2. After reading Ephesians 6:10–20, describe the essential elements of a Christian's campaign against Satan and his fallen angels.

3. Compare 1 Timothy 3:6 with Revelation 12:9–10. What sins led to the downfall of Satan and his ouster from the courts of heaven? What did Jesus say about that day in Luke 10:17–20? What important lessons can we learn from these biblical references?

4. Describe the two mistakes Christians often make when appraising the strength and tactics of their spiritual enemy, the devil. Which do you think is the most costly mistake in the matter of rescuing the lost?

5. Describe the three "alerts" sounded in this session for Christians engaged in spiritual warfare. Why is it important for Christians to know the enemy?

6. What is the importance of the advice in James 4:7–10 ? How does this apply to the old saying, "If God seems far away, guess who moved"?

Session 4 An Attitude of Gratitude

The Lord is an excellent strategist. As evidence, consider the battle which Gideon and 300 men fought against the Midianites. The Bible says Gideon was opposed by "all the sons of the east [who] were lying in the valley as numerous as locusts and their camels were without number, as numerous as the sand on the seashore" (Judges 7:12 NASB). (When you are outnumbered a-thousand-to-one an exact count is unimportant.)

Initially the odds were not so lopsided. In fact, the Bible tells us 32,000 men responded to Gideon's call to arms. But God thought having so many soldiers would be detrimental in the long run. If they won such a battle, the Israelites would be tempted to think the victory was accomplished by their own strength. The Lord told Gideon to allow any who were afraid to go home. What a strange thing to do. (I'm surprised Gideon was not numbered among those who left.) When the dust had settled, 22,000 headed home, and only 10,000 remained. Still too many. After the Lord's final cut, Gideon's army numbered only 300 soldiers. How could so few conquer so many? That is where divine strategy comes into play.

First, God strengthened the faith of Gideon by allowing him to overhear an enemy soldier's prophetic dream. Thus fortified, he distributed a trumpet, torch, and clay jar to each of the 300 men who remained. The he divided his band into thirds and surrounded the camp of the enemy. At Gideon's signal the men were told to break their pots, display their torches, and blow their trumpets. Seeing their camp surrounded, the enemy was thrown into panic. The Midianites grabbed their swords and began slashing away in the darkness. God's strategy had worked perfectly as Israel's enemies literally destroyed themselves in the darkness.

Things are not always as they seem. The Midianites were convinced they had been encircled by a superior force. As Christians we, too, are outnumbered by those who dwell in darkness. Our cause seems hopeless, but things are not always as they seem. God's strength is best seen in weakness.

The Witness of Christian Harmony

I couldn't help but think of the Concordia University System as I read the story of Gideon. Our numbers are not so great, but we have 'em surrounded. Concordia campuses are located all over the country: as far east as Bronxville, N.Y.; as far west as Irvine, Calif., and Portland, Oreg. Although not a traditional stronghold, Concordias are found south in Selma, Ala. and Austin, Tex. Concordia, Seward, Nebr., is strategically placed in the heartland. And if you prefer more northern climates, you can take your pick of locations at Ann Arbor, Mich., Mequon, Wisc., River Forest, Ill., or St. Paul, Minn. Our Concordias seem to be everywhere!

The Concordia concept is a great witness to Christian unity. During a recent state gathering of pastors and lay leaders in Concordia, Mo., I couldn't help but think about the concept of calling all our schools by one and the same name. In the chapel of the Lutheran high school at Concordia hung a banner dominated by a globe of the world, with a sash unfurled across its equator. Words on the sash read "Living in Harmony." At the top and bottom of the banner was the school's name and a Scripture reference: "St. Paul Lutheran High School—Romans 12:16." The school, being located in a town called *Concordia* was clever in establishing "Living in Harmony" as their motto, for that is what the word *Concordia* means. The Bible passage confirmed the theme.

> Live in harmony with one another. Do not be proud, but be willing to associate with people of low position. Do not be conceited. (Romans 12:16)

The Power of Light

God's strategy for winning battles has not changed from the time of Gideon. Although outnumbered, Gideon's soldiers surrounded the Midianites with their torches flaring in the darkness. They actually used darkness to their advantage, for by contrast the Lord's army was plainly visible. The enemy panicked and was soon overwhelmed.

Today the Lord asks His followers to "let your light shine before men, that they may see your good deeds and praise your Father in heaven" (Matthew 5:16). Light and darkness cannot coexist. When one enters the room the other must leave by necessity. Darkness and light are not equals. Whenever light appears darkness flees. Darkness cannot overcome light. Darkness may surround a small flickering light and make it feel insignificant and ineffective in vast darkness, but it can never be so dark that light cannot be seen. Just the opposite is true, the darker the night the more visible the light. Darkness may try to keep light from expanding its influence, but wherever light is found, darkness must give way.

When Christians live their lives in harmony (as citizens of *Concordia*) their witness cannot be denied or overcome by the world. Jesus said, "A new command I give you: Love one another. As I have loved you, so you must love one another. By this all men will know that you are my disciples, if you love one another" (John 13:34–35).

Others will come to know that we are God's children by the attitude that we bring to our lives. When our lives are lived in gratitude for all that He has done for us, He is glorified. When we forgive others as we have been forgiven, He is glorified. When we are patient and kind to those who do us harm, He is glorified. When we give no quarter to false teachers out of love for those they mislead, He is glorified. When we use all our means and devote our time and energies to help others overcome life's hardships, He is glorified.

Faith in the Workplace—Walking the Talk

Hector is a man after Gideon's heart. Wherever he goes the light shines. I first met Hector as I stood greeting the worshipers as they filed by me after the morning service. Over my shoulder in the narthex I kept hearing a cheerful voice saying, "Good morning. I'm Hector and this is my wife, Debbie, and our daughter Cammie." He was "out-greeting" our official greeters. That moment defines Hector and his attitude for life. The fact that he was of Hispanic heritage in a mostly Anglo environment didn't dim his light even a little.

Needless to say, Hector became a good friend, and I learned to appreciate how his winsome spirit was applied to life in all its forms. His family relocated to St. Louis when Hector assumed a senior position in a major corporation whose headquarters were located in our area. When he hosted a meeting of all the regional vice-presidents, along with the CEO and other corporate brass, Hector asked if anyone would like to open the meeting with prayer! A friend gently advised that corporate meetings weren't typically begun with prayer, to which Hector responded, "I didn't get this far without it, and I'm not about to change now. Gentlemen, allow me this moment." And they did.

Once, when asked to negotiate a multimillion dollar settlement with another international corporation, Hector assured his CEO that all would be fine. "Jehovah and I will take care of it" was the message he left on the voice mail. Later, when he reported on the success of the meeting, his superior asked him who Joe Hava was, and when did he come to work for the corporation. After some confused moments, Hector realized his voice-mail message about Jehovah was misunderstood … but not for long.

Not everyone can be a Hector. Our personalities don't always lend themselves to being so transparent. All Christians are called to be a witness however and to take their stand for Jesus the Savior. The Holy Spirit dwells in our heart (1 Corinthians 12:3) and can enable Christians to live in the world without conforming to the world. Our witness then becomes a beacon of hope to those living in the dark and shadowy world of the lost. Paul called it our "spiritual act of worship."

> Therefore, I urge you, brothers, in view of God's mercy, to offer your bodies as living sacrifices, holy and pleasing to God— this is your spiritual act of worship. Do not conform any longer to the pattern of this world, but be transformed by the renewing of your mind. Then you will be able to test and approve what God's will is—His good, pleasing and perfect will. (Romans 12:1–2)

Control, Control, Who's Got Control?

Many people go through life letting external conditions control them. Early in our marriage Carol and I were prone to that faulty thinking, of the opinion that when things changed around us then life would improve. You know how that thinking goes:

- If we only made $150 more per month, we could keep our budget in the black.
- If we lived in a bigger city, there would be more opportunities for evangelism.
- If and when our boys were both in school, life could return to normal.
- If I looked a little older I'd get more respect from those I'm trying to lead.

It's amusing now to look back on those days. Over time we have come to realize that it is not our circumstances that control us, but our attitude about our circumstances. Paul spoke of this attitude-adjustment and called it "the secret of being content." Here is how he described it,

> I know what it is to be in need, and I know what it is to have plenty. I have learned the secret of being content in any and every situation, whether well fed or hungry, whether living in plenty or in want. I can do everything through Him who gives me strength. (Philippians 4:12–13)

People who practice Paul's secret will stand out from the rest. Their light will be visible and draw others to the faith that enables them to be positive in a negative world. The old proverb is not far from the truth: An optimist believes a thing can be done while a pessimist believes it can't, and they are both right.

Our optimism isn't without basis. As the old hymn affirms: "My hope is built on nothing less Than Jesus' blood and righteousness"! Paul wrote, "If God is for us, who can be against us? He who did not spare His own Son, but gave Him up for us all—how will He not also, along with Him, graciously give us all things?" (Romans 8:31–32).

Christianity Is Not a Denial of Reality

Living a positive life in a negative world is not an act of denial. The three young men who were arrested and threatened with death if they would not bow down to the false god that Nebuchadnezzar had erected in Babylon were fully aware of the consequence. They took a public stand for their faith with no special word from God that they would be spared. Their story is a classic example of faithfulness in adversity.

> Nebuchadnezzar said to them, "Is it true, Shadrach, Meshach and Abednego, that you do not serve my gods or worship the image of gold I have set up? Now when you hear the sound of the horn, flute, zither, lyre, harp, pipes and all kinds of music, if you are ready to fall down and worship the image I made, very good. But if you do not worship it, you will be thrown immediately into a blazing furnace. Then what god will be able to rescue you from my hand?"
>
> Shadrach, Meshach and Abednego replied to the king, "O Nebuchadnezzar, we do not need to defend ourselves before

you in this matter. If we are thrown into the blazing furnace, the God we serve is able to save us from it, and He will rescue us from your hand, O king. But even if He does not, we want you to know, O king, that we will not serve your gods or worship the image of gold you have set up." (Daniel 3:14–18)

The phrase *But even if He does not* was an extremely bold profession of faith by Shadrach, Meshach, and Abednego. Clearly the three young men were unaware of what God was planning, nor did it matter to them. They would be faithful regardless of the outcome. No denial here. They were fully aware of the real possibility of their pending death. Their faithfulness was based on the certain hope of eternal life, not a fair-weathered belief that so long as life is good, God is worthy to be honored and His Word kept sacred. Belief in Christ is not a denial of reality. The Christian faith provides peace, love, and joy in the midst of reality.

Sometimes the Way Is Narrow

Not only do Christians encounter the same difficulties and uncertainties of life that mark the lives of nonbelievers, they may encounter additional difficulties because of their faith—just ask any faithful Christian teenager.

Peer pressure is great at any age, but adult Christians have the luxury of picking and choosing their friends. High school students on the other hand live in a world assigned to them by virtue of their birth date, family status, and the school district in which they reside. To live faithfully in such an environment is like building a fire in the rain, the conditions are not conducive to success. The assault can be relentless.

Christian teens encounter all the teenage temptations to insecurity, promiscuity, alcohol, and substance abuse. They especially know what Paul meant when he concluded in frustration

I know that nothing good lives in me, that is, in my sinful nature. For I have the desire to do what is good, but I cannot carry it out. … So I find this law at work: When I want to do good, evil is right there with me. For in my inner being I delight in God's law; but I see another law at work in the members of my body, waging war against the law of my mind and making me a prisoner of the law of sin at work within my members. (Romans 7:18, 21–23)

51

But perhaps even greater than the war "within their members," is the war other teenagers wage to "snitch-proof" their circle of friends. In the world of the American teenager, the noncompliant teen is considered one of the greatest threats to the freedom they have come to know and to love.

The initial assault comes in an all-out attempt to bring about compliance. Teens that are smoking, drinking, and engaging in inappropriate sexual activity are some of the most persuasive persons you will ever meet. The temptation to join the "enlightened" and break free from the naiveté of adolescence is a powerful lure. In this new and intimidating world, the desire to find acceptance (especially among older and more established peers) is an almost irresistible attraction. Christians who remain faithful to the Lord in their teen years will likely find His values unwelcome in their new surroundings. The possibility of standing alone during life's most social hour is more than many can bear. Christian teens who compromise their faith find it hard to attend youth Bible studies, listen to sermons (no matter how interesting), or even be very honest with their parents. It can be a guilt-laden time for those who succumb. And those who maintain the narrow path will find fewer invitations to hang out, date, or party with their classmates. How well I remember singing the old hymn "Jesus! And Shall It Ever Be" with a twinge of conscience as a Christian teen.

Jesus! Oh, how could it be true,
A mortal man ashamed of You?
Ashamed of You, whom angels praise,
Whose glories shine through endless days?

Ashamed of Jesus, that dear friend
On whom my hopes of heav'n depend?
No; when I blush, be this my shame,
That I no more revere His name.

Lights Are Meant for Dark Places

Of course, Christian teenagers aren't the only ones whose love for Christ makes love for the world impossible. Single adults and those who work in a job that daily tests the limits of faith know the struggle, too. As Jesus said, no one can serve two masters (Matthew 6:24). If there was any doubt about compatibility between this world's standards and the standards of the Lord, John's comments in his first letter will make the matter clear.

> Do not love the world or anything in the world. If anyone loves the world, the love of the Father is not in him. For everything in the world—the cravings of sinful man, the lust of his eyes and the boasting of what he has and does—comes not from the Father but from the world. The world and its desires pass away, but the man who does the will of God lives forever. (1 John 2:15-17)

Christians aren't perfect, except in the righteousness they receive by grace through faith in Jesus. Living in a nonbelieving world will undoubtedly cause Christians to slip, stumble, and fall from time to time. But failure in our walk doesn't have to mean our defeat. On the contrary, it provides another opportunity to do the unexpected and turn a mistake into a victory for Christ.

More than 10 years ago I received a card in the mail from an anonymous Christian. I never discovered who wrote it, nor do I remember the reason behind her story, but it is a good example of how the love of Jesus can turn a loss into a gain.

> Pastor,
>
> I wrote a letter to you quite a while back, talking of and about your church and what I thought you preached and about a certain member who also taught a class and of her behavior.
>
> I feel now I was in the wrong for doing such a thing. I am not to judge you or anyone else. I hope you will forgive this rude deed on my part.
>
> I know not what you teach or preach, but I do know that Christians are known by the fruits that they bear—and that we can be "fruit inspectors." If we are the Christians Christ would have us to be, we will bear the fruit of the Spirit. This is what I want for my life for sure! Although I don't see this in everyone who claims to be a Christian, I do hope and pray to have this for myself, and hope I can set a better example of Christ's love in me to those around me.
>
> I do hope and pray for your forgiveness in this matter. I will pray for you and your ministry.
>
> > In His Love,
> > A Fellow Christian

Our life is meant to be a witness to the lost and an encouragement to the saved. When Paul urged Christians to keep up the practice of regular worship, it was for the reason of mutual encouragement.

Let us hold unswervingly to the hope we profess, for He who promised is faithful. And let us consider how we may spur one another on toward love and good deeds. Let us not give up meeting together, as some are in the habit of doing, but let us encourage one another—and all the more as you see the Day approaching. (Hebrews 10:23–25)

Faithful in a Little, Faithful in Much

When a job is too big to be tackled all at once it helps to remember the little slogan Inch by inch, this job's a cinch. The same could be said for living the Christian life with an attitude of gratitude. In the parable of the talents Jesus used this natural principle to make a spiritual point when He said, "Well done, good and faithful servant! You have been faithful with a few things; I will put you in charge of many things. Come and share your master's happiness!" (Matthew 25:21).

The job of boldly living the Christian faith before a nonbelieving world is not done all at once, nor are the hard decisions made in a vacuum.

In a commencement speech made in 1993, President Ronald Reagan reminded his audience of the principle of consistency. The September 1995 issue of *The Working Communicator* quotes him as follows:

For you see, the character that takes command in moments of crucial choices has already been determined. It has been determined by a thousand other choices made earlier in seemingly unimportant moments. It has been determined by all those "little" choices of years past—by all those times when the voice of conscience was at war with the voice of temptation—whispering a lie that "it doesn't really matter." It has been determined by all the day-to-day decisions made when life seemed easy and crises seemed far away—the decisions that piece by piece, bit by bit, developed habits of discipline or of laziness; habits of self-sacrifice or self-indulgence; habits of duty and honor and integrity—or dishonor and shame.

Christians know that the only power strong enough to overcome the world and enable them to live consistent lives of faith, is the power of the Holy Spirit working through God's almighty Word. The same Word that commanded light to appear out of darkness can transform an ordinary life into an extraordinary witness. The miraculous transformation is in itself another testimony to the glory of God. Paul said,

> For God, who said, "Let light shine out of darkness," made His light shine in our hearts to give us the light of the knowledge of the glory of God in the face of Christ.
>
> But we have this treasure in jars of clay to show that this all-surpassing power is from God and not from us. We are hard pressed on every side, but not crushed; perplexed, but not in despair; persecuted, but not abandoned; struck down, but not destroyed. (2 Corinthians 4:6–9)

Too Big to Be Small

Booker T. Washington, the great educator and founder of Tuskegee Institute in Tuskegee, Ala., once complimented his mentor by calling him, "too big to be small." When Christians demonstrate the fruit of the Spirit, which is "love, joy, peace, patience, kindness, goodness, faithfulness, gentleness and self-control," they will amaze those who observe them as being "too big to be small."

Not only does such an attitude draw attention to the motive for such behavior (which is Christ), it also benefits the Christian who lives his or her faith with integrity. James wrote,

> Do not merely listen to the word, and so deceive yourselves. Do what it says. Anyone who listens to the word but does not do what it says is like a man who looks at his face in a mirror and, after looking at himself, goes away and immediately forgets what he looks like. But the man who looks intently into the perfect law that gives freedom, and continues to do this, not forgetting what he has heard, but doing it—he will be blessed in what he does. (James 1:22–25)

When Christians hear the Word but do not practice their faith, they have only a shallow faith of the intellect. In his famous work *Law and Gospel,* C. F. W. Walther said people who live such a life, "Labor under a grievous self-delusion. People in that condition have nothing but the dead faith of the intellect, a specious faith, or, to express it still more drastically, a lip faith."

By contrast, Christians who hear *and* practice the Word will be blessed in what they do. Their own faith will deepen, and they will become more useful servants to the Lord. On that great and final day, Christians who have lived such a life will be surprised to hear their Master say, "Well done, good and faithful servant! You have been faithful with a few things; I will put you in charge of many things. Come and share your master's happiness!" (Matthew 25:21).

For Discussion

1. How was Gideon's battle against the Midianites similar to our war against the enemies of faith and the temptation to conform to the world?

2. How is it possible to live a positive Christian life in a negative, post-Christian world?

3. What do you think is the main lesson we can learn from Shadrach, Meshach, and Abednego?

4. Do you agree that being a faithful teenage Christian is probably the hardest of all witnesses in our American culture? What can be done to help people in such difficult stages of life?

5. What did the author mean when he said that hard decisions are not made in a vacuum? What was the main point of Ronald Reagan's speech and how can it be applied to living a faithful Christian life?

6. According to the quotation from James 1 and the reference to Dr. Walther's observation about faith of the intellect, how does the Christian benefit from the daily exercise of their faith?

Session 5 The World Has Changed

The late Charles Kuralt, American traveler, reporter, and author once said, "Thanks to the Interstate Highway System, it is now possible to travel across the country from coast to coast without seeing it." His irony is telling, but there is more about America that goes unseen than the countryside. Almost everything about our nation is changing, and changing fast. So fast in fact, many changes fly by the citizenry largely unnoticed. We have ears but we're not listening. We have eyes but there is much that we do not see.

As evidence, consider the communication revolution. Twenty-five years ago I dated a red-headed college girl who actually owned her very own typewriter. I was impressed. It locked neatly into its own case so we could carry it from dorm to dorm. The portable feature wasn't so important until she discovered I had taken typing in high school. From then on she did less typing and I did more carrying. I remember thinking how privileged she was to own her own portable machine.

The reign of manual-portables passed like gas through a teenager's car. They were soon replaced by faster electric models. Wow! With a flick of a switch it purred like a big cat ready to pounce on its prey. With hardly a touch a good typist could orchestrate a deafening rapid-fire attack. That was power. What a weapon! Simple typing unleashed explosions that turned heads and gathered crowds. At seminary I proudly owned an electric-portable that used pop-in-cartridges with different colored ribbons and correction tape—the end of white-out! My second congregation owned new IBMs, which used the famous "spinning balls." These babies enabled the same machine to produce different styles of type in either elite or pica font. Secretaries spread foam-rubber pads at their work stations to protect the delicate teeth of their new magic spheres. What innovation! We "desktop-published" bulletins in three or four different type-faces. The congregation was amazed to see the quality of our work.

After that changes came in a blur: Typewriters developed memories that stored several lines of work before striking the paper. (Why?—I don't know.) Then came word processors, mainframes, personal computers, laptops, and now small electronic notepads able to run CD-ROM, modems, portable printers, and fax machines. Did I mention e-mail and the World Wide Web? It's safe to say I won't be needing those last few sheets of carbon paper in my desk drawer anytime soon.

Secretaries can empathize with Dorothy upon her arrival in Oz. "Toto," she said, "It doesn't feel like we're in Kansas anymore!" Dorothy awoke to discover Oz was just dream, a nightmare of illusion. Pinch yourself all you want, this reality is not going away.

The World Has Gotten Smaller

The world has changed, and for many reasons, including communication and ease of transportation, it has gotten smaller. Before I journeyed off to college, I could honestly say the farthest I had traveled from home was a one-time family vacation into the neighboring state of Michigan. My sons, by contrast have visited countless states, the nation's capital, been to the ocean several times (we live in St. Louis), climbed mountains in Colorado, and canoed the boundary waters of Minnesota. Last January I traveled to Russia on a mission trip, and next spring my oldest son will spend a college semester studying in India. Did I mention that the world has gotten smaller?

Who Is Coming to America? Who Is "Everyone"?

Neil Diamond described the waves of immigrants coming to America in his song entitled "America."

According to a recently released study of the world populations published by Dr. Robert Scudieri of the Board for Mission Services of The Lutheran Church-Missouri Synod, the world would look like this if it were a village of 1,000 people:

By continents, there would be
- 564 Asians;
- 210 Europeans;
- 86 Africans;
- 80 South Americans;
- 60 North Americans.

By religions, there would be:
- 329 Christians;
- 174 Muslims;
- 131 Hindus;
- 61 Buddhist;
- 52 animist;
- 3 Jews;
- 34 believers in other sects and religions;
- 216 people with no identifiable religious belief.
  In this village
- 60 people would have half the income (note: the same number of Americans in category 1 above);
- 500 people would be hungry;
- 600 people would live in shantytowns;
- 700 people would be illiterate.

Dr. Ed Wescott, the former LCMS Director of World Missions used to say, "The Lord wanted us to bring the Gospel to the peoples, but we were slow to go. So, He sent the peoples to us!" In his new work, *What Effective Churches Have Learned,* George Barna sounds an alert for the American Christian community. According to The U.S. Census Bureau (1995 data), Caucasian domination of America will diminish substantially in the years to come, falling from 76 percent of the population in 1990 to just 52 percent by the year 2050. By contrast, the Hispanic population will rise from 9 percent to 22 percent, and the Asian population, almost nonexistent a generation ago, will comprise 10 percent of the nation.

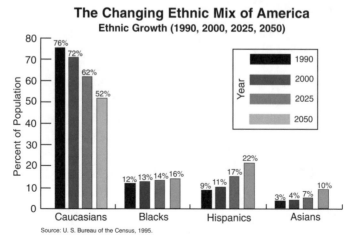

The Changing Ethnic Mix of America
Ethnic Growth (1990, 2000, 2025, 2050)

Source: U. S. Bureau of the Census, 1995.

The Effects Are Beginning to Show

Occasionally the changes occupy the media spotlight and Americans are forced to deal with them. When a young man by the name of Mahmond Abdul-Rauf refused to rise for the singing of the national anthem, it got America's attention. Abdul-Rauf is not an Arab living in America protesting allegiance to a foreign flag. Abdul-Rauf is an NBA basketball player under contract to the Denver Nuggets for $2.6 million per season—about $31,000 per game. He was born and raised in Mississippi under the name of Chris Jackson. Before he became Abdul-Rauf, Chris Jackson was a member of a Southern Baptist congregation. Our children don't have to travel around the world to be exposed to the powerful influences of non-Christian beliefs. Neither do we have to visit remote corners of the globe to share the Christian faith with the world. As Neil Diamond says in a popular song, "They're coming to America." America has changed, and you haven't seen anything yet!

Who are the Muslims, Hindus, Buddhists, and New Agers and what do they believe?

A Quick Overview of this New World

Muslims. Muslims are the followers of Islam, which literally means "submission." They live in submission to their god, Allah, as he is revealed in the Koran, the sacred book of Islam. Muslims honor five dogmas, or supreme pillars of faith: (1) Muslims are unitarian. They believe Allah is the only true and eternal god, and he created all things. (2) Muhammad was the final and most important prophet sent by Allah. He came in succession after the four previous and therefore lesser prophets: Noah, Abraham, Moses, and Jesus. (3) The Koran is the written word of Allah dictated to Muhammad by the angel Gabriel in the month of Ramadan. (4) The angels (of which Gabriel is chief) were created before the world and are of greater substance than anything known to man. (5) There will be a Last Day (a Judgment Day) in which the works of the faithful will earn them heaven and those who fall short will be consigned to one of seven levels of hell. The one unpardonable sin, and the worst offense, is to associate with any deity other than Allah.

Muslims will be judged on the basis of how faithfully they maintained the Islamic faith, which requires the following: (1) Verbal profession of no god but Allah. (2) Daily observance of five obligatory prayers at dawn, noon, midafternoon, sunset, and night. Prayers are to be said after certain preparations and then in a posture facing Mecca, the birth place of Muhammad. (3) Almsgiving. (4) Fasting during the month of Ramadan; the faithful are not to eat or drink from dawn to sunset. Allowance can be made for the feeble, the sick, and those traveling. (5) A holy pilgrimage to Mecca at least once in a lifetime. A stone that supposedly fell from heaven (some think a meteor) is ensconced there, which on Judgment Day will give witness to all who kissed it, thus proving their pilgrimage.

Hinduism. The Hindu faith is an ancient belief that originated in India before the time of Christ. Its adherents total more than 400 million people worldwide including 70 percent of the Indian population. The name is believed to have been derived from a tribe of people who lived along the Indus river. The Muslim invaders later referred to all the country as Hindustan, and its people as Hindus.

The Hindu faith is not a doctrinal faith in the same way as Judaism, Christianity, or Islam. It recognizes no one sacred book, and its most ancient writings are not written to reveal truth or god, but offer formulas for personal spiritual discovery. The Hindu faith rests on *karma* (literally, "action deeds") which a believer produces to progress toward total "enlightenment" and an eventual and final merger with the infinite. This progression is not accomplished in one lifetime, which explains why the Hindu faith places such emphasis on reincarnation in many and varied life forms, including animals and human life at various levels or "castes" in society.

Although Hindus may talk of many gods, their faith is established chiefly on the worship of Brahma (the creator), Vishnu (the sustainer), and Siva (the destroyer). They believe that their gods can and sometimes do take human form called avatars. Mahatma Gandhi, Rama, and Krishna are said to be an examples of this phenomena. The religious practice of the faith involves spiritual exercise (yoga), which is intended to help a person commune with god through the chanting of praises, also called mantras. Modern-day teachers, or spirit guides, are called gurus. These spiritual masters are highly honored in Hindu society, as they counsel and "coach" their followers toward greater divine consciousness.

New Age movement. If Hindu beliefs seem strikingly similar to the New Age movement, you are beginning to understand the extent of Hinduism's influence. Gurus of the New Age are called "channelers." Like the old-age avatars, they are used by gods (even possessed by ancient gods) to grant enlightenment and bring adherents into harmony with the universe. New Agers believe that when enough people transcend their physical limitations and achieve total consciousness, then a new age of perfect harmony will be ushered in. It is not surprising that reincarnation and talk of previous lives is an essential element of the New Age movement. Like its Hindu predecessor, the New Age movement teaches that life is a means of progression toward unity with the infinite. Many even believe that between incarnations spirits may actually choose their future life conditions (fully aware of coming hardships, disease, and struggles) as experiences needed to assist in their ultimate goal of spiritual progression.

Although they may speak of Christ, New Agers do not teach that Jesus' death accomplished forgiveness of sins for His followers. Christ is reduced to an example of self-denial who provided a worthy model of life leading to total spiritual transformation. They believe Jesus' death was not substitutionary and had no saving effect except as evidence that the physical world cannot tolerate a spiritual person.

Buddhism. Many Americans are familiar with the smiling bronze statutes of Buddha but most know little about who he was or why he is smiling. The founder of Buddhism is a man named Siddhartha Gautama. He was born in India about 560 B.C. but rejected the Hindu faith with its emphasis on social castes and suffering as necessary steps toward total enlightenment. Siddhartha believed self-denial, not suffering, was the path to victory. As a teacher of this new way, Siddhartha changed his name to Buddha, which literally means "enlightened one."

He taught that spiritual victory is only achieved when life ceases with no more reincarnations. He called the state of nonexistence Nirvana, which literally means "blowing out."

Buddha's teaching is based on four noble truths:
- The universality of suffering
- The unenlightened man clings to desire, which leads to suffering
- Self-denial is the key to freedom from desire and suffering
- Through enlightenment self-denial can be achieved

63

The path of enlightenment for a Buddhist is based on 10 commandments of self-denial: (1) no taking of life; (2) no theft; (3) absolute celibacy; (4) no lying; (5) avoiding liquor; (6) no eating—except between sunrise and noon; (7) the avoidance of the arts (i.e., dancing, theater, and music); (8) no jewelry or perfume; (9) no sleeping on raised beds; and (10) no possession of gold or silver. Buddhists are to live lives of absolute poverty, practicing virtues of benevolence, patience, and humility. The Buddhist faith, like Hinduism, believes that truth is experienced not taught. Buddha did not believe in the existence of a soul, gods, or fixed truths. Some would argue that Buddhism is nothing more than a form of enlightened atheism, a philosophy of life which teaches self-denial as the highest quality of human existence.

How Do We Witness in This Strange New World

Although not inspired, Dale Carnegie offers some timely advice on the subject.

> I taught debating and argumentation in New York; and once, I am ashamed to admit, I planned to write a book on the subject. Since then, I have listened to, engaged in, and watched the effect of thousands of arguments. As a result of all this, I have come to the conclusion that there is only one way under high heaven to get the best of an argument—and that is to avoid it. Avoid it as you would avoid rattlesnakes and earthquakes.

Point 1—Avoid Arguments

Carnegie's advice may not be inspired, but it has support in the Scriptures.

- "Starting a quarrel is like breaching a dam; so drop the matter before a dispute breaks out. … He who loves a quarrel loves sin; he who builds a high gate invites destruction." (Proverbs 17:14, 19)
- "It is to a man's honor to avoid strife, but every fool is quick to quarrel." (Proverbs 20:3)
- "Without wood a fire goes out; without gossip a quarrel dies down. As charcoal to embers and as wood to fire, so is a quarrelsome man for kindling strife." (Proverbs 26:20–21)

Solomon in his wisdom would first advise us to resist the temptation to argue. Not only should we avoid being argumentative, neither should we allow ourselves to be drawn into an argument by those to whom we are witnessing. It takes two to argue, and as Solomon observed, a fire without fuel remains small and soon burns out. Our words have greater impact if we refrain from argumentation.

Point 2—There Is No Need to Be Defensive

Solomon advised the righteous to lower their walls and listen to those who disagree with them. (See Proverbs 17:19 above.) This does not mean the truth of the Christian faith is subject to debate, or that Christians should lessen their conviction. Having confidence in the truth of God's Word, mature Christians can engage those of different faith without fear of different viewpoints. Remember it is the Holy Spirit's job to convert the lost, not ours. Solomon compared those who lacked confidence to a city that builds a high gate. Those who exhibit a defensive posture invite attack. If we are willing to talk calmly and without fighting we stand a better chance of being heard. Christians have no cause to be defensive. The truth of God's Word (remember session 2) does its own fighting and doesn't need to be, nor can it be, empowered by our debating skills.

Point 3—Develop a Reputation for Gentleness and Respect

Avoiding arguments is not the same as avoiding all discussion of the Christian faith. Much Scripture could be cited which urges the faithful to always be ready to give an account of the hope that is within them. They key point here is not *what* you share, but *how* you share your personal convictions. The old axiom is right, People don't care what you know if they don't know that you care. Peter reminded the first-century Christians to gain the respect of their audience by godly behavior so that later, if any would speak ill of them, the kindness of their example would support their witness.

> Who is going to harm you if you are eager to do good? But even if you should suffer for what is right, you are blessed. "Do not fear what they fear; do not be frightened." But in your hearts set apart Christ as Lord. Always be prepared to give an answer to

everyone who asks you to give the reason for the hope that you have. But do this with gentleness and respect, keeping a clear conscience, so that those who speak maliciously against your good behavior in Christ may be ashamed of their slander. (1 Peter 3:13-16)

Point 4—You Have Not Failed if They Walk Away

One of the hardest things a Christian will ever experience is rejection. Not personal rejection, but rejection of the Gospel— especially by those we love. When we believe that there is no other name given among men by which we must be saved except the name of Jesus, then rejection of the Gospel means rejection of salvation (Acts 4:12). Jesus predicted the heartache when He said, "Do not suppose that I have come to bring peace to the earth. I did not come to bring peace, but a sword. For I have come to turn 'a man against his father, a daughter against her mother, a daughter-in-law against her mother-in-law—a man's enemies will be the members of his own household' " (Matthew 10:34–36).

When as children we memorized the Commandments, we never realized the full implications of the first and greatest of the 10. In His own explanation, the Lord describes Himself as a jealous God. The Hebrew word is *kan-naw*. In this case, *The Living Bible* actually does a better job of translating the sentence by saying, "I, the Lord your God am very possessive, I will not share your affection with any other god!" (Exodus 20:5). God is possessive of us. Jesus said, "I give [My own] eternal life, and they shall never perish; no one can snatch them out of My hand. My Father, who has given them to Me, is greater than all; no one can snatch them out of My Father's hand" (John 10:28–29). That passage is a great comfort when we think of all the evil things that could tempt us to set aside our Christian faith. The same passage doesn't seem so wonderful when

- the challenge to faith comes from an aged father living in another state who has never professed saving faith;
- our heart is tied to Jewish parents who feel rejected because their child has married a Christian spouse and accepted Jesus as the Messiah;
- we prayerfully consider the fate of a wayward child whose lifestyle is a rejection of all that is sacred and holy;
- going to church means going alone because your spouse would rather play golf than attend church and Sunday

school with their family;
- a friend just doesn't understand how we can let the "church" control our lives and make demands on our time, energies, and finances.

These are not rare or isolated occurrences. Every Sunday the pastors in the congregation I serve invite our worshipers to come forward for personal prayer after each service. Every Sunday one or more of those prayer requests is about a loved one who is living outside of the saving grace of Jesus Christ.

If it hurts you to see those you love risk eternity for other earthly priorities, how must it hurt the Savior? In our liturgical responses we sing words that Peter spoke to Jesus in John 6:68. Whenever I sing them I think about the pain Jesus was feeling at that time. The Lord had just taught a very difficult lesson about the saving nature of His body and blood. Many who had been following Him could simply not accept such bold claims and began to walk away. Jesus did not chase them down the street in an attempt to better explain what they had misunderstood. Instead, He turned to the Twelve and asked, "Will you also leave Me?" Peter answered for them all. "Lord, to whom shall we go? You have the words of eternal life" (John 6:68). I have never considered Peter's response a strong affirmation. I imagine him thinking, "Lord, we don't understand any better than those who just walked away, but for some unexplainable reason, we know You are right. You are always right. You are the Savior." He was walking by faith, not sight (2 Corinthians 5:7).

Point 5—Be Persistent without Being a Pest

We are called to witness, only God can make the convert. Jesus told His own disciples to expect rejection as well as acceptance. Then He reminded them, "He who listens to you listens to Me; he who rejects you rejects Me; but he who rejects Me rejects Him Who sent Me" (Luke 10:16). Knowing his friends and loved ones rejected God (and not him personally), didn't make the apostle's pain any less painful. Paul wrote about his personal agony, saying, "I have great sorrow and unceasing anguish in my heart. For I could wish that I myself were cursed and cut off from Christ for the sake of my brothers, those of my own race, the people of Israel" (Romans 9:2–4). He went on to affirm what all Christians must believe, "It is not as though God's Word had failed. For not all who are descended from Israel are Israel" (Romans 9:6).

67

God's Word does not fail. Every time it is unleashed it goes forth with power. As Christians it is not up to us to be so convincing and winsome that we will "trick" people into the Kingdom. We are called only to be faithful, gentle, and respectful as we speak of the hope that is within us. Keep the faith and keep making your witness. Today is the day of salvation, not the day of judgment—not yet (John 3:17; 2 Corinthians 6:2).

Although Solomon was talking about personal initiative and goal setting, the wise king has also provided an excellent strategy for witnessing to a changing world. "Sow your seed in the morning, and at evening let not your hands be idle, for you do not know which will succeed, whether this or that, or whether both will do equally well" (Ecclesiastes 11:6).

For Discussion

1. How have the changes that the author mentions affected your life? How have you experienced "the world getting smaller"?

2. Do you agree with Dr. Wescott's statement, "The Lord wanted us to bring the Gospel to the peoples, but we were slow to go. So He sent the peoples to us"? What implications does that statement have for you and your congregation?

3. What effect does the U.S. census data have on you? What impact, if any, does it have on the way we conduct our congregational ministries?

4. In what ways is the New Age movement similar to Hinduism and Buddhism? In what ways are all non-Christian religions similar?

5. Explain the difference between contending for the faith and being contentious? Was Carnegie right about the uselessness of arguing and debate? Why or why not?

6. Based on the Bible passages cited and the suggestions of the author, what advice would you offer to those called to witness to those who have rejected Christ for another way of life?

Session 6 Mission Values, and Vision

The denomination of which I am a member has a wonderful heritage of mission, outreach, and doctrinal integrity. No generation can rest on the reputation of those who have gone before. George Washington said, "The price of freedom is eternal vigilance." The price of maintaining our church's heritage is continued commitment to the great commission of Jesus Christ!

At a recent gathering of pastors the discussion turned to the marks of the true church which led to an affirmation of Article VII of the Augsburg Confession of 1530.

> It is also taught among us that one holy Christian church will be and remain forever. This is the assembly of all believers among whom the Gospel is preached in its purity and the holy sacraments are administered according to the Gospel. For it is sufficient for the true unity of the Christian church that the Gospel be preached in conformity with a pure understanding of it and that the sacraments be administered in accordance with the divine Word. It is not necessary for the true unity of the Christian church that ceremonies, instituted by men, should be observed uniformly in all places. It is as Paul says in Eph. 4:4, 5, "There is one body and one Spirit, just as you were called to the one hope that belongs to your call, one Lord, one faith, one baptism."

We stand firmly on the bold proclamation asserted by Martin Luther that lost and condemned sinners are saved by grace through faith alone!

Our congregation has developed a concise mission statement to help us maintain our heritage and our focus on the great commission of Jesus. It simply states,

Our Mission
Our mission is to save the lost and strengthen the saved to live bold and courageous lives of Christian witness before a nonbelieving world.

We have also developed 8 guiding values and 12 vision statements to better focus how God's mission will be carried out among us.

Our Values

X 1. We believe the congregation is not the mission. It is established by God to accomplish the mission (1 Corinthians 9:22, Philippians 2:1-4).

2. We believe God's truth is revealed with power in His inerrant Word (2 Peter 1:20-21; Isaiah 55:10-11).

3. We believe faithful Christian ministry will emphasize salvation by grace through faith in Jesus Christ (Ephesians 2:8-10; 1 Corinthians 2:2).

4. We believe followers of Jesus Christ will demonstrate good works and the fruit of the Spirit which is: love, joy, peace, patience, kindness, goodness, faithfulness, gentleness, self-control (Galatians 5:22-23; Matthew 7:16).

5. We believe that every Christian is called by God to live a life of eternal significance and is uniquely gifted for service (Romans 12:1; 1 Peter 4:10).

6. We believe integrity, not popularity, is God's standard for faithful Christian leaders (Isaiah 51:7,8, Galatians 1:10).

X 7. We believe that God is creative by nature and innovation, without compromise of truth, is God-pleasing (John 14:12, Isaiah 43:18-19).

X 8. We believe that God is honored by excellence in ministry (Ecclesiastics 9:10; 1 Corinthians 9:24-27; 2 Peter 1:5-11).

Our Vision

(Compelled by our mission and guided by our values, we shall endeavor to:)

X 1. Worship the Lord in spirit and in truth (John 4:24; Hebrews 10:23-25).

2. Honor the Lord with biblically faithful and culturally relevant teaching (2 Timothy 4:1-5).

X 3. Inspire God's people to share their faith naturally and eagerly (Acts 4:19-20; 1 Peter 3:15).

X 4. Provide a variety of opportunities for Christians to grow spiritually through the regular study of God's Word (1 Peter 2:1-2; Hebrews 6:1-3).

5. Honor the Lord with music and song, praising Him with psalms, hymns, and spiritual songs (Psalm 33:1-4, Ephesians 5:19-20).

6. Provide Christian care and counseling to help carry each others burdens (Galatians 6:2; Matthew 25:34-36).

7. Provide excellence in the Christian education of God's children (Proverbs 22:6; Deuteronomy 4:4-7).

8. Encourage, train, and equip young people to live faithful lives in their youth (Ecclesiastes 11:9-10; 1 Timothy 4:12).

9. Conduct a ministry of intentional influence beyond our community and support mission endeavors near and far (Luke 12:47-48; 24:46-47).

10. Identify and equip spiritual leadership among lay and professional servants of the Lord (Ephesians 4:11-12; 2 Timothy 1:6-7).

11. Maintain our facilities as good stewards of God's gracious gifts (Haggai 1:4-5; James 1:17).

12. Provide opportunities for Christian fellowship and mutual encouragement (Hebrews 10:23-25).

Our Four-Fold Expectation of Members

1. To be faithful in regular worship, prayer, and participation in the sacraments established by God for the spiritual uplifting and encouragement of His people (Exodus 20:8; Hebrews 10:25; 1 Corinthians 11:26).

2. To be faithful in regular Bible study, both personal and corporate (Luke 11:28; 1 Peter 2:2-3; Hebrews 6:1-3).

3. To be faithful in living lives of eternal significance (James 1:23-25; Romans 12:1-2; 1 Corinthians 6:19-20).

4. To be faithful in the financial support of the Lord's work (Malachi 3: 8-12, Matthew 23:23, 2 Corinthians 9:6-15).

The divine mission is given to Christians by God. Your values (the priorities of your ministry) and your vision (the aspects of Christian ministry which you will emphasize) may be different than ours, and rightfully so. In different places, and different times the strategy for conducting ministry may change, but the means of grace—the Word and Sacraments—remain God's unchanging way of accomplishing His purpose in every place and time.

God expects us to serve Him. We are not placed on earth and redeemed by God to simply enjoy life and pay our bills. As Martin Luther said, "Jesus Christ ... has redeemed me, a lost and condemned person, purchased and won me from all sins, from death, and from the power of the devil; not with gold or silver, but with His holy, precious blood and with His innocent suffering and death, *that I may be His own and live under Him in His kingdom and serve Him in everlasting righteousness, innocence and blessedness*" (emphasis added).

A banner that hangs in one of the main meeting rooms of Concordia University in Irvine, California, reminds all who see it to live the faith they profess.

> God has given me this day to use as I will. I can waste it or use it for good. What I do today is important, because I am exchanging a day of my life for it. When tomorrow comes this day will be gone, forever living in its place something I have traded. I want it to be gain, not loss, good, not evil, in order that I may not regret the price I paid.

Forming Your Strategy

Dr. A. L. Barry has established an effective, Christ-centered strategy for The Lutheran Church—Missouri Synod. His mission statement is clear: "Keep the message straight, and get the message out." What is the motive for the mission and for his personal life of Christian witness? There is no need for speculation. Under every signature at the end of his correspondence you will find a reference to Jude 24–25. Those who take the time to look the passage up will learn that Jesus and the salvation He has freely provided is the driving force of Dr. Barry's life and ministry. It is an effective way for any Christian to capture the curiosity of another and direct them to the gospel of Jesus Christ.

In addition to Dr. Barry's overriding mission of faithfulness and proclamation, he has outlined a strategy for the conducting of the mission. It is a fivefold statement of his vision for the Church. (1) Be strongly in the Word. (2) Be people sensitive and people centered. (3) Reach out boldly with the gospel. (4) Be faithful to the Scriptures and the Lutheran Confessions. (5) Let our work be marked with peace and unity. It is a good strategy and helps him and those around him focus their work for the mission of Jesus Christ among us.

What is your mission strategy? Adlai H. Rust, one of the founders of State Farm Insurance reminded his associates of their primary purpose with a mission statement that now hangs as a reminder in thousands of offices nationwide.

> Wherever we serve ourselves but not our customer, we will in time serve no one. Wherever we put first the sure performance of our duty to the policyholder, we will surely succeed.

> But there is more to a happy and successful career than just money. There are the satisfactions and rewards that come … from the good that you do for your fellow man.

Take the time to consider the examples shared in this session to formulate your own personal mission statement. Can you identify a scriptural passage that would be a constant reminder of your mission for Christ?

The verse assigned by Pastor Sheppman at my confirmation was from 1 John 1:8–9, a good reminder of God's grace and readiness to forgive. The passage that guides my life and work however is taken from Joshua 1:7, "Be strong and very courageous. Be careful to obey all the law my servant Moses gave you; do not turn from it to the right or to the left, that you may be successful wherever you go." As a pastor this verse is significant because I identify strongly with Joshua's inadequacy. He was asked to assume the leadership of God's people in the place of Moses who had served so effectively the previous 40 years. The waiting was over, the unconquered land lay before them, and Joshua was called to lead. God soothed his concern and provided a twofold strategy for success. (1) Be strong and courageous. (2) Never compromise the Word.

Personalizing the Mission

Is there a biblical character or verse that you might study to help you in your unique service to the Lord? You may have noticed how in our fourfold expectation of our congregational members we ask each person, "To be faithful in living lives of eternal significance." In years past our congregation, like most, tried to involve new members on some board, committee, or another aspect of service, perhaps as a teacher in our Sunday school. The prevailing view was that such involvement would cement their relationship to the congregation and assure their continuation as a faithful and committed member. There is an element of truth to that strategy and every congregation needs a certain number of members to assume various tasks and functions within the organization. Such an attitude can also innocently teach the wrong idea that work on behalf of the membership is the highest form of Christian service. Remember our first value statement? "We believe the congregation is not the mission. It is established by God to accomplish the mission."

We believe that each Christian has a unique and vital role in the kingdom of God. It may be to serve their fellow members within the congregation, but it may not be. We reorganized our congregational structure under the slogan "Get God's people out of meetings and into ministry." Involvement and useful service is important, but it doesn't have to be sitting around a church table until 10:30 P.M. in the fellowship hall. Many members cannot attend regularly scheduled meetings and carry needless guilt about their inability to serve. No one would argue that the Lord's expectation of young mothers, traveling executives, and people who work weekends or at night is any less than for those who live a more routine existence. Maybe their service will take the form of bringing a lonely widow to worship services, reading daily devotions with an elderly neighbor over the phone, or serving on a nonprofit urban renewal board. Christians should be challenged to think creatively about ways to serve the Lord by serving others. Volunteering in a city hospital can be a very vital way to live your life for Christ. Our congregation no longer considers it our responsibility to tell Christian members how they ought to serve the Lord, but we do ask them to identify at least one way in which they are involved in something of eternal value—an act of Christian mission. The result has been that many people are now initiating new and innovative forms of Christian service. They recruit their own support and conduct whatever meetings they need at times convenient to those involved. The result has been infectious. Many small-group Bible studies now have a mission project as an additional reason for meeting.

Developing Skills for Lifestyle Evangelism

Mark Twain once said, "Thunder is wonderful, thunder is impressive, but it is lightning that does the work." I have spent fruitless years trying to teach that truth to my dog Sarah, who hides under our bed every time thunderstorms rumble past our country home. She still has too great a regard for thunder.

The same message must be shared with those who think the things they do contribute to the salvation of anyone. Only God saves by the power of the Holy Spirit working through the efficacious and inerrant Word. Paul took no credit for the growth that occurred in Corinth, and he was quick to correct faulty thinking about the source of true spiritual growth.

What, after all, is Apollos? And what is Paul? Only servants,

through whom you came to believe—as the Lord has assigned to each his task. I planted the seed, Apollos watered it, but God made it grow. So neither he who plants nor he who waters is anything, but only God, who makes things grow. (1 Corinthians 3:5-7)

We cannot make the Word of God anymore powerful than it already is by our skill and technique. We can however inhibit and frustrate the work of God by being careless or hypocritical in our life of Christian witness. Pastor Rick Warren is the senior pastor of the fastest-growing Baptist church in American history, located in the Saddleback Valley of Southern California. His church grew from just one family to more than 10,000 people in worship in just 15 years. As you can imagine, Pastor Warren has much to say about the techniques of effective Christian witness but he is absolutely firm on this point: "Only God grows the church!" He begins each day with the prayer, "Father, I know You're going to do some incredible things in Your world today. Please give me the privilege of getting in on some of what You're doing." In other words, (Warren writes) church leaders should stop praying, "Lord, bless what I'm doing: and start praying, "Lord, help me to do what You are blessing."

It Is Not What's New That Works

If conversion of sinners is God's work, we can assume it is not a new thing. It is not what is new that works, it is what has always worked. The church is built on the foundation of the prophets and apostles, with Christ Jesus as the chief Cornerstone (Ephesians 2:20). It has always been that way and always will be. Any other kind of growth is like a house built on shifting sand—it simply will not stand the test of time and will certainly be destroyed in the coming storm of Christ's final judgment.

The Bible says that faith comes by hearing, namely hearing the gospel of Jesus Christ (Romans 10:17). Whenever Christians tell others what Christ has done through His life, death, and the victory of His resurrection the possibility for conversion exists. It does not mean that every time Christians share the Gospel conversion will occur. But it does mean that every time the Gospel is shared the person to whom we are speaking must deal with God. The Word of God always goes forth with power. It is not the words we use, or the smoothness of our presentation, but the message itself that changes hearts. In all my years of Christian witnessing, some of the most amazing conversions I've observed came only after a lost sinner literally dragged the Gospel out of an inarticulate and hesitant Christian through their own sincere and probing questions.

The Gun Won't Fire if You Don't Pull the Trigger

I'm an avid white-tail deer hunter, as are my two sons. Every November you will find us up before dawn, clothed in florescent orange, trying to keep warm while waiting for the right buck to pass within shooting distance of our tree stands. The first year my sons joined me in the hunt, my youngest missed several opportunities before shooting the largest deer of the season. His first shot clicked harmlessly—on an empty rifle. He had safely climbed the tree with an empty gun and had failed to ready his firearm. In a quick attempt to chamber a shell, he failed to clear the bolt and jammed the rifle. Needless to say that deer quickly bounded away to safety. You can be in the right place at the right time, have the right equipment, but still need to know how use it.

Will Rogers once said, "Having the world's best idea is not any good unless you act on it. People who want milk shouldn't sit on a stool in the middle of a field and hope that a cow will back up to them." You need to pull the trigger or the gun won't fire. Christians need to unsheathe the sword—the Word of God—if they expect to do battle in the kingdom of the Lord.

If it is difficult for you to share your faith, plan to spend some time with someone more experienced.

Our congregation is located close to our denomination's largest seminary, and as a result we have student-pastors assigned to our congregation for practical experience. Rarely have I met a student who didn't panic at the prospect of one-on-one personal ministry. Standing in front of a room full of people is less frightening to them than the thought of talking personally with someone about matters of great spiritual importance. I have also noticed how quickly that fear subsides and how excited the same students can become after they have accompanied me or another pastor on a few personal visits. Nothing overcomes inexperience like experience. If you find conversations about spiritual matters difficult, ask to make some visits with your pastor or a fellow Christian who has been making visits for a number of years. If your pastor is hesitant to make visits, maybe he has never had the benefit of the experience which you or another seasoned evangelist could offer in a respectful and sensitive way.

The Best Guides Know the Area

When hunting, canoeing, or fishing in new territory you can buy detailed maps and books to guide you. They are of some help, but the best guide is someone who knows the area. Likewise, it is important that those who desire to lead others to the pleasant pastures of the Lord spend some time there themselves.

I know of a pastor who created quite a stir in his congregation when he urged the passage of motion limiting membership on boards and offices of the church to those who were faithfully participating in Christian Bible study. The same thing happened when our congregation made it an expectation of elders that they make monthly visits on the membership of the congregation. While Christian congregations always want to guard against legalistic enforcement of manmade rules, it stands to reason that those introducing others to the Gospel of Jesus Christ would have more than a passing knowledge of the Bible and the value of prayer. A wise man once said, "If you want passionate people in your organization— be passionate. If you want committed people in your organization— be committed. If commitment isn't important—be mediocre." The only things of eternal consequence are spiritual matters. Christians can't afford to treat them as insignificant, or give the Lord's work less than their best effort.

Ralph Emerson said, "Every great and commanding moment in the annals of the world is the triumph of some enthusiasm." To be enthusiastic literally means, "to be possessed by God." Paul said, "Christ's love compels us, because we are convinced that one died for all, and therefore all died. And He died for all, that those who live should no longer live for themselves but for Him who died for them and was raised again" (2 Corinthians 5:14). Paul was possessed by God. He no longer viewed his own life as something over which he had control. He was compelled, constrained, controlled, driven, and directed by the love of God. This was not an attitude restricted to apostles and first century Christians. Paul said it should be the same for everyone for whom Christ died and rose again.

Our life is a living testimony to those things we hold most dear. Priorities are revealed naturally by the places people go, the things they do, the way they treat others, the issues they discuss, and the expenditure of their resources. Christians are no different. It was impossible for Paul to think any other way. He said, "I have been crucified with Christ and I no longer live, but Christ lives in me. The life I live in the body, I live by faith in the Son of God, who loved me and gave Himself for me" (Galatians 2:20).

Lifestyle evangelism is allowing others to routinely see the motivation, prevailing attitudes, and priorities of the Christian life by means of the everyday activity of those who are no longer secret disciples of Jesus Christ. Lifestyle evangelists have taken up the cross to follow Jesus, and in so doing *"dared to be different."*

For Discussion

1. Analyze the strengths of your congregation. What are some of the best ways your congregation can reach others with the Gospel of Jesus Christ? What are your own personal strengths and how can they be used to further the kingdom of the Lord?

2. Do you have a personal mission for the Lord, i.e., something that you do for Jesus that has the potential of reaching the lost with the saving news of Jesus' love?

3. Look up Jude 24–25. Take time this week to choose a verse of your own and memorize it. Perhaps you could begin to use it in creative ways next to your signature.

PS 139 23:24

4. What's the hardest thing about sharing the Gospel with people one-on-one? Analyze the approach of someone you know who seems to talk more openly about their faith. Are there lessons we can learn to help us be more natural in this important work?

5. Why is it important to remember that we can add nothing to the saving power of the Gospel by our approach or strategy? Do you think it helps or hurts to have good "sales experience"?

6. What are some things you could do to be less secretive about your relationship to Jesus Christ? What are some things you could do to gain confidence in your ability to talk about spiritual things?